# Worship:
## Beyond the
## Hymnbook

# Worship: Beyond the Hymnbook

## A Communication Specialist Looks at Worship

Charles H. Kraft

Foreword by
Chuck Fromm

WIPF & STOCK · Eugene, Oregon

WORSHIP
Beyond the Hymnbook
A Communication Specialist Looks at Worship

Wipf and Stock
An Imprint of Wipf and Stock Publishers
199 W. 8th Ave., Suite 3
Eugene, OR 97401

www.wipfandstock.com

ISBN 13: 978-1-62564-869-3

Manufactured in the U.S.A.                              01/16/2015

# Contents

# CONTENTS

# Foreword

I MET CHUCK KRAFT in 1977: First through his groundbreaking book, *Christianity in Culture: A Study in Biblical Theologizing* and then in person through a mutual friend, John Wimber. At the time John was working both with us at Maranatha! Music and at Fuller Evangelistic Association. Chuck Kraft was a professor of anthropology and intercultural communication at the School of World Mission (now School of Intercultural Studies) at Fuller Theological Seminary in Pasadena. Next to the Bible, John Wimber would say, "Professor Kraft's book was the most personally thought-provoking impacting book on my life."

Now, in this long-awaited book on worship, Chuck calls pastors to new accountability and sounds a clarion call to all believers. Simply put, Chuck believes that churches were built for worship, so that is what should happen there. He says, "I believe worship should be talked about. If worship is important to God, pastors ought to preach on it fairly often, and Sunday School teachers should teach on it. There should be much attention given in church to worship attitudes, rituals, times, places, and styles."

Chuck says this emphatically and proceeds to do just that. Something he's been doing for quite some time, actually. Chuck Kraft's explication of incarnate communication impacted my vision of and for worship significantly and was a game changer and a worship shaper for many. Though he is not known primarily as a worship scholar, certainly worship is the apex of his focus on incarnational communication. As Chuck expresses so eloquently, Christian messages are "person messages," not simply "word messages" and the only totally appropriate media for these messages are human beings. Since the way God communicates is person to person, it stands to reason that is the way he prefers us to communicate with him. If that's all I, or anyone, received from Chuck, it would be significant.

But not only did Chuck move us from the conceptual to the enacted in worship, from mind-speak to heart-talk and artful communication, but he foreshadowed the current emphasis we see in books such as Vertical Worship. Chuck addressed these themes in the early issues of *The Worship Times*, a journal that was the forerunner of *Worship Leader Magazine*. I look back to the very first issue we published where Chuck moved us beyond mental constructs to active verbs—beyond the noun worship to actually worshiping. He makes us aware of the importance of language in our relationship with God.

This is a book in part about Chuck's own personal worship revolution and revelation and the larger one that shook the foundations of the institutional church and supplanted the pipe organ with the guitar and replaced antiquated and formal language with heartfelt declarations of love in the vernacular with the advent of overhead projectors and screens and the demise of books that held hands and eyes captive. It also charts the opportunities inherent in worship communication for true spiritual formation and the ever-present possible pitfalls. And the truth that every preaching pastor must know: a congregation may not remember your sermon, in fact probably won't, unless it is connected to the sung worship, which they most likely will remember.

My dear friend gives us vocabulary, concepts, and criteria for experiencing and evaluating worship. Like Mary McGann, he looks at worship from many vantage points. He sees as an anthropologist, communication specialist, theologian, observer, and participant, and in so doing, he teaches us to do the same. Chuck is passionate about worship and worshiping, and in writing this book, his hope is to spread his passion and multiply it till the sound of spiritual awakening fills the whole earth.

Chuck Fromm

Editor of *Worship Leader Magazine*

August 2014

# Introduction

WORSHIP IS ONE OF the most important things human beings can do, not because it feeds God's ego but because it lines us up with him against our enemy, Satan. Worship is an act of war. It is also an act of participation, strengthening our relationship with God and with each other. Satan cannot stand worship. He hates us, especially when we partner with God to exalt God and to state our position with him.

In worship we declare that we are on God's side. We declare this to God, to ourselves, to other people, and to the spirit world. These declarations, then, are acts of communication. And communication happens according to rules that God has put into the universe.

In the mid-eighties I was asked by Chuck Fromm, then director and eventually owner of Maranatha! Music to write a regular column in a publication he had started named, *Worship Times*, dealing with worship and communication. This I gladly did, and continued to do for several issues of *Worship Leader*, the successor to *Worship Times*.

The chapters that follow are the articles written for the two journals referred to above. I have slightly edited some of them but mostly they are as they were. They are not in the same order as they were written. I have arranged them according to subject rather than chronologically. There is some repetition due to the overlapping of the subjects. I hope the reader will forgive me for this.

In addition to those articles are three items I have added that were not printed in either *WT* or *WL*. They relate to an article written by Donald Hustad and published in *Christianity Today*. Fromm asked me to respond to that article, since Hustad takes a different point of view on our subject. The article is entitled, "Let's Not Just Praise the Lord." Fromm and I felt *CT* owed us the chance to counter Hustad's position by presenting our views on the subject. So, I wrote the article, submitted it to *CT* and it was rejected. *CT* did, however, offer me the opportunity to write a very short (less than one page) piece stating my position.

I have included as appendix A Hustad's article, as appendix B, my long response and as appendix C my short response. The longer response has never been published, disappointing us by not using my article to balance Hustad. Before reading these chapters, the reader might want to read Hustad's article followed by my responses.

My own background, sometimes evident in the chapters, is as a traditional non-charismatic evangelical who has become (since 1982) what might be labeled "semi-charismatic." So, much of what I write here is directed to non-charismatic evangelicals rather than to those raised on "contemporary worship." I have gone through a paradigm shift myself from hymnbook worship to overhead (or PowerPoint) worship and would like to help those who, like Hustad, are fettered by tradition and missing the renewal God has been orchestrating through contemporary worship.

*I believe contemporary worship is the most important thing God has brought into Christianity in our day, especially for those of us who have become "dry" in our traditional evangelical churches.* Through contemporary worship, many of us have grown out of the intellectualism that plagues our Christianity into a much more meaningful relational experience.

I have been asked twice when invited to preach if I wanted to make any changes in what we would do on Sunday morning. My suggestion was that we do the most important thing last—that we get the teaching part (sermon) out of the way early and then do what we said we came for: worship. These experiments went well, especially in Hong Kong in 1994 where the topic of the sermon was to be "What do we do in Hong Kong when China takes over in 1997?" We had one or two songs as we gathered. Then I spoke from some of the persecution passages of the New Testament suggesting that when Paul and his associates were put in prison, they looked aAround, they looked up and, in the face of persecution, they celebrated (Acts 16:25). When my sermon was over, the worship leader took over, they pushed the chairs back and we sang and danced (worshipped) for the next hour or more.

Christianity is all about relationship. These chapters are intended to feed your relationship with Jesus. Picture him with you as you read. Experience the one who turned his back on "organ Christianity" in favor of "guitar Christianity" (see chapter 12). And may God bless you as you read.

South Pasadena, CA
August 2014

# Shouldn't We Be Teaching People How to Worship?

### Teaching Jimmy, Part 1

"Worship at 11:00," the sign said. Five-year-old Jimmy was just learning to read and had been able to pronounce the words on the sign outside the church. "What's worship, Mommy?" he asked. "That's what we do in church," she answered. But Jimmy had never been allowed to stay through "big people's church." So his mother's answer didn't satisfy him. "Could I stay to see?" he asked. "If you'll be quiet," she replied.

An important part of Christian faith and practice depends on what we communicate to the next generation. Jimmy wanted to find out what worship is. So his mother let him stay. But what did he learn?

Jimmy found what he saw and heard to be quite interesting. Various people stood up on the platform and talked. Was this worship? Jimmy soon found out that it wasn't okay for him to talk, though, even to ask what was going on. Because everybody else seemed to be quiet, Jimmy decided a person apparently had to be quiet to worship. Every once in a while, though, all the people stood up to sing. And once, a group of people sitting on the platform sang. Was the singing worship? Sometimes everyone bowed their heads and prayed. Was that worship? And toward the

What is worship?

end, the pastor stood up and talked for a long time. Was that the worship part? Or was all of it worship?

We might chuckle at the way what we call a "worship service" looks to a five-year-old. But how is Jimmy going to find out what this part of life is all about? Perhaps on the way home Jimmy would ask his mother if everything that went on in church was worship. How would his mother answer him? Would she even know?

The sermon was the central part of the service. Yet *not one of the 800 or more references to worship in Scripture equates preaching with worship.* And worship is mentioned about three times as often as preaching. Indeed, in the Scriptures we find that *though preaching is for now, worship is forever.* We say we are following the Bible. But are we? Will Jimmy be able to learn what the Bible means by worship and how important worship is by observing what we do on Sunday morning? Would Jimmy's mother be able to define worship?

I'm afraid most of those attending our "worship services" would be hard put to come up with an adequate scriptural definition of worship. Instead, we tend to assume that everyone understands what worship is. And *people seldom talk about what everyone assumes.* Worship, therefore, is seldom talked about and seldom taught on. I doubt, for example, that I have heard three sermons on worship (I can't remember one) in more than sixty years of churchgoing. The church I presently attend is probably ahead of most, however, in that it has scheduled one seminar and one Sunday school class on the topic in the past twenty-five years.

> Preaching is for now, worship is forever.

Since we know that *meanings are assigned by the receivers of messages on the basis of their experience,* it is likely that most of our people assume that what we do in church is what God wants us to do. They probably think worship-less meetings like that observed by Jimmy are what worship services are supposed to be.

But how will they learn anything different? Where are people taught how to worship? Is learning to worship supposed to be a "do-it-yourself" project? Or can people be taught?

I believe worship should be talked about. If worship is important to God, pastors ought to preach on it fairly often, and Sunday school teachers should teach on it. There should be much attention given in church to worship attitudes, rituals, times, places, and styles. And people should be led

We should teach what worship is.

to practice. How can we expect people to know what worship is all about if it is not communicated to them?

## What to Teach

Worship is primarily about *allegiance* and *relationship*. When people do what they do to express worship, they are demonstrating their commitment to whomever or whatever they are worshipping. Wherever Abraham, Isaac, and Jacob went, they built altars at which they expressed their allegiance to the Lord (Gen 12ff). Moses was told to lead Israel out of Egypt so they could demonstrate their commitment to God without Egyptian interference (Exod 7ff). The Sabbath was to be honored by setting it aside for worship (Lev 23:3). The tabernacle, and later the temple, were to be places of worship, where the people expressed their allegiance to God, exhibiting their relationship with God.

In Daniel's day, the people were commanded to bow down in worship before the image of gold that had been made by Nebuchadnezzar (Dan 3:1–7). Isaiah saw flaming creatures surrounding God's throne calling out "Holy, holy, holy," and worshipped in response (Isa 6:1–4). In the book of Revelation, John records several examples of worship (e.g., Rev 4:6–11; 5:8–14; 7:10–12; 11:16–17, etc.). Several times in Jesus' ministry Scripture records that people whom he had healed expressed their allegiance to him by worshipping him (e.g., Luke 8:35; John 9:38).

In such examples, we hear words of commitment and honor spoken, songs of praise sung, and postures of reverence adopted. The holiness and worthiness of the Lord is proclaimed in word and song. People and angels kneel and prostrate themselves. In the pictures of heaven, the heavenly beings seem to spend long periods at worship. Expressions of adoration and gratefulness are prominent, with the worshippers losing themselves in the process.

Worship in Scripture often seems to be noisy, as in Isaiah when "the sound of their voices made the foundation of the Temple shake" (6:4). On that occasion, the worship even involved smoke. On other occasions, it involved incense and harps (Rev 5.8), lightning (Rev 4; 5; 11:19), and earthquakes (Rev 11:19).

What does contemporary worship involve? What of Scripture has been communicated to present generations? How will Jimmy learn? Who will teach him (and his mother)?

# 2

# Teaching Jimmy, Part 2

Jimmy is twelve now. He has graduated from junior church, been through the New Members' Class, been baptized, and joined the church. During the membership class he was taught about doctrine and the history and distinctives of the denomination, but nothing about worship. Though many of Jimmy's peers have left the church, he's quite serious about his Christian commitment and has stuck with the church. But he still carries subconsciously many questions about the meaning of some of the things that are done in church.

Singing, for example. When Jimmy was small, they used to do fun singing in junior church. They sang a lot about Jesus and how much he loved children. Then when he got to attend grownup church more often, he found the singing dull, with the people reading all the words from hymnbooks. Recently, though, things had begun to change in their church. Many of the songs were now projected on an overhead projector. And more instruments were used, even guitars and a drum. Those songs were peppier, shorter and easier to remember—more like what they used to do in junior church.

Jimmy's parents didn't particularly like the change, though. They had to learn new words and tunes, they complained. And sometimes the music got loud and people clapped their hands so it didn't seem like church anymore. They admitted that the younger people (and even some of the older ones) seemed to like the new approach better but wondered what might happen to the giving if the older folks got turned off. But still nobody raised the question of what worship really is all about.

Neither Jimmy nor his parents have been helped to ask the most basic questions. And now they come out at opposite ends of the spectrum with regard to musical preference and only know how to state their preferences. They have no standard or criterion by which to measure what ought to be. They can only discuss what is and what each prefers.

## Meaningful Ritual

I have stated that worship is primarily a matter of allegiance. Add to that, relationship, the aim of allegiance. If so, we need to ask what feeds and strengthens allegiance and relationship? The answer lies in the building of habits that strengthen the intended commitment. Group habits are called rituals. In our family we have regular rituals to celebrate birthdays and holidays. My wife is a master at making sure that our children and their families get together as often as possible. This strengthens our relationship with each other enormously, not because we do spectacular things but because we do a variety of meaningful things together.

Though ours is not a family without problems, ours is a family in which each is committed to the others and all of us to God. As we feed those commitments, we honor each other and worship our God. Much of what we do is the same or similar each time. Among our rituals are barbequed meat, homemade ice cream, birthday cakes with quarters in them, special dishes brought by daughters and daughters-in-law and prayer before meals. But there's variety too. The birthday cakes are often different shapes, there are often new foods, frequently new jokes, a different person is featured for each birthday and there are new things to observe and talk about as the children move into different stages of life. And both the repeated things and the new things are sacred. The biggest enemies of such commitment are neglect and meaninglessness. Allegiance and

What feeds and strengthens allegiance and relationship?

6

relationship have to be cultivated. If we neglect getting together, our family falls apart.

The same is true for our relationship with God. This is why Jesus spent so much time with the Father. If we neglect spending time with the other members of our church, our relationships fall apart. This is why we are told by the author of Hebrews not to neglect getting together as Christians (10:25). Jimmy and all the rest of us need to be taught to see and experience church as family. This is extremely difficult when the buildings we meet in and nearly everything we do in them tends to depersonalize. Probably more allegiance to each other and perhaps, also to God is expressed in the informal, personal interactions in the foyer after church than in any part of the "worship service."

The other thing that can ruin family and church relationships is to regularly engage in activities that are meaningless or that have negative meaning. We are warned by Jesus against "vain repetition" (Matt 6:7). Though the primary reference here is to meaningless words, the danger is just as great for meaningless ("vain") activities. These can kill relationships in family or church. What, then, do Jimmy (and his parents) need to learn?

> We need to experience church as family.

They need to give primary attention to the meaning of worship. Jimmy needs to do the things that carry the proper meanings. The founder of Young Life, Jim Rayburn, used to say, "It's a sin to bore a kid." Let's not bore Jimmy.

# 3

# Teaching Jimmy, Part 3

In the last two chapters we raised the question of what we are communicating to the next generation concerning worship. Five-year-old Jimmy couldn't figure out what worship was even after attending a meeting called a "worship service." Nor could his mother. Let's picture Jimmy at about fifteen now. His days in junior church are over and he attends adult church regularly. If he was your son, how would you help him understand worship? Following are some possibilities:

   1. *Worship is expressing reverence and honor to God.*

This would be a good place to start. The word worship and the words worth and worthy derive from the same root. Worship, then, can be seen as our attempt to express to God how great he is and how worthy to be exalted and praised. As the psalmist says, "Your greatness is seen in all the world" (8:1) in creation (both in nature and in how he has put humans together), in sustaining the universe, in redeeming, forgiving, and accepting us and in countless other ways.

Worship is our attempt to express how worthy God is.

In worship, we are to recognize his greatness, his goodness, his love and all of the marvelous things he has done that warrant our commitment to him and his kingdom. If we attempt to teach Jimmy this facet of worship, will what he experiences in church reinforce the message? He learned that he had to be quiet in church. Will he know that this is to show respect and honor to God? The songs sung exalt God. Does he get the point? The preacher speaks very respectfully about God. But does any of this get beyond Jimmy's head into his heart? Hopefully. But Jimmy, like everyone else, will need both to "do" worship and to have things explained if he is to understand.

2. *Worship takes time.*

As when we honor humans, we need to take time at it. Expressing important things, whether reverence or love, can seldom be done quickly. As in lovemaking, the meaning and value of the experience is badly damaged when the time is shortened. Worship is meant to be done slowly and, like lovemaking, with constant awareness of the mystery of the interaction. This mystery often reduces us to silence but also involves moments of exultation.

Will Jimmy learn this in church? In many churches, the words used may be just right but the time expended is simply too short. We cannot really "get into it" before we have to turn to the next item on the schedule. One of the saddest things about what we do in church is our enslavement to the clock. The shortness of time expended in worship is one of Satan's most useful tools to keep us from getting close to God. Jimmy may learn that time is more important than worship.

3. *Worship is an exciting right and privilege, not a duty.*

It is a function of who we are—second only to God in creation (Ps 8:5) as well as of who God is. Though we are to see the Lord "high and exalted" (Is 6:1), we are invited to approach God's throne boldly, with confidence (Heb 4:16), because we belong there, like grandchildren come to grandma's house. Will Jimmy learn to get excited about worship? Will he see it as a right or a routine? We were made for worship, we were redeemed for worship. What a tragedy if we never find this out.

> We are invited to come to God boldly.

4. *To worship, one must be involved.*

Meaningful expression cannot be reduced to mere ritual and retain its meaning. Ritual (a form of habit) is an amazing thing: we need enough of it to feel comfortable, but not so much that it becomes a meaningless routine. As with lovemaking, going through the motions gets it over with but leaves one very unsatisfied.

I find that picturing enables me to get involved. Our hymns, praise, and worship songs are rich with imagery that can be pictured as we sing or meditate. I picture the thirsty deer, the seeking Shepherd, the majestic Lord, the manger scene, Jesus teaching his disciples. Others use other techniques to get involved in worship. Will anyone teach Jimmy what the possibilities are in this regard? Or will we let him experience worship as mere routine?

5. *Worship is to be a shared experience.*

Though we can and should worship alone, sharing a ritual usually increases its meaning and value. We are made for relationships with others as well as with God. Worship of God with others feeds both relational needs. Healthy family dynamics may instruct us here. When spouse honors spouse, it is good. But when children gather together to honor a parent, it is extra special, both for the one honored and for the children. When we gather in corporate worship God is thrilled. So should we be.

Will this fact be gotten across to Jimmy? Will he know he's part of a family of worshippers and how meaningful that can be? How will the next generation (or our generation) learn what worship is supposed to be if we don't talk about it. I would contend that worship is the most important thing we do in church. If so, how would anyone ever discover this truth?

Worship is the most important thing we do in church.

6. *Finally, worship is an act of war.*

See the following chapters for a discussion of this factor.

# 4

# Worship As Warfare, Part 1

WE'VE BEEN ATTEMPTING TO teach Jimmy (representing the next generation) what worship is all about. So far we've focused on some very important aspects of what he needs to know and express on the human level. But there's another dimension so important, and so neglected, that it deserves special emphasis. Jimmy needs to know that *worship is warfare*. And this fact should be a major part of what we teach our children about worship. But there is more to be said.

There are many dimensions to warfare. Among them are the need for *protection from the enemy*. When we worship, we enable our God to do more of what he wants to do than would have been true otherwise. God seems to have made a rule for himself that he will not work in the human arena without a human partner. Worship of a spirit being activates a law of the universe to this effect—enabling the spirit being (God) to do what he wants to do.

When we worship we enable God to do more of what He wants to do.

Praising God seems to erect a spiritual barrier that the enemy cannot get through. When we worship in church, those enemy spirits whose job it is to harass and attack us cannot continue their work on us, at least during the time we are worshipping. The expression of our commitment to God in that corporate setting and in a place sanctified through dedication and continual usage to honor God protects us from their harassment.

One reason the enemy likes to disrupt worship is to protect his interests. Say, for example, someone is living in sin, worshipping insincerely, distracted or refusing/neglecting to participate in the worship. Though the enemy has a good grip on this person, worship interferes with the enemy's activity in that person. The enemy does not leave, but he cannot do what he wants to do during that time, especially if the person is worshipping "in spirit and in truth" (John 4:23).

In private, then, continually singing God's praises has the same protective effect, and with the same qualifications mentioned above. Continually worshipping in spirit and in truth prevents, or at least hinders, the enemy from doing what he wants to do with/in us. The worshipper is in a kind of "spiritual bubble" (like a plastic container) with enemy spirits outside it trying to get in but failing because of the worship barrier between them and the worshipper.

People who live in a state of worship receive constant protection, whether driving, walking, working, or carrying out their functions at home. People who neglect or forget to worship are vulnerable to the enemy's attacks to the extent that their internal weaknesses allow him to connect with them. John 14:30 points out that Jesus could not be bested in such attacks because Satan could not find anything in him that gave him the right to do his work on Jesus. When we have things within us that give the enemy such a right, worship hinders him when he tries to come at us.

> People who neglect worship are vulnerable to the enemy's attacks.

One exciting thing about contemporary worship music is that it is often easy to memorize. This provides us with a convenient way to keep the praise of the Lord continually "flowing" in our hearts and minds (Ps 34:1). That continual flow, beyond the uplifting effect it has on our spirits, is protective. It reinforces the spiritual bubble and keeps the enemy at bay. The use of older hymns for this purpose is equally effective, but they are often less easily memorized and thus, in general, not quite as convenient.

Memorization of praise and worship songs, whether the newer or the older ones, that incorporate Scripture is especially helpful since enemy spirits do not function well in the face of God's Word. Satan and his spirits like to harass and attack us at home also. Thus, it is excellent strategy to have praise and worship music playing continually in our homes. As in church and in our individual lives, though, it is necessary that the "container" be first cleansed of anything that gives the enemy rights to it if the protective value of the worship is to be maximized. That is, our home should be prayed over in the authority of the owner of the house and Jesus to break any power of enemy spirits over the house, the land, and any artifacts in the home that may have been dedicated to evil spirits (e.g., as is true of certain traditional objects we bring home from visits to societies in which spirit worship is practiced).

Young Jimmy would be way ahead of where most of us were at his age if we taught him such things as these early in his life. Perhaps the majority of American Christians have no idea we are at war. They do not, therefore, understand that they are gaining protection whenever they worship, much less see worship as the important factor in warfare that it really is. Let's not let Jimmy go as long as most of us did without learning this.

# Worship as Warfare, Part 2

"STOP THAT MUSIC, STOP that music. I can't stand that music!" It was the voice of a demon that couldn't stand the Christian music being played on an organ by a pastor's wife as the pastor was challenging him. He couldn't stand the praise that was being lifted to Jesus even though it was just the music being played without the words to the hymns she was playing.

If Jimmy is to have a good grasp of what worship is, he needs to also deal with worship as warfare. Hopefully, his pastor recognizes that worship challenges our enemy. Most pastors don't seem to know this and, therefore, don't deal with this fact. But those who deal with the spirit world recognize this truth. That's why the above pastor had his wife tormenting the demon by playing Christian music.

Why would a demon be upset over the simple playing of Christian music (on an organ, no less!)? It is because, as the demon said, they can't stand praise and worship of their enemy—God. Many things are not clear concerning what is going on in the spirit world. But an example like this one gives us a clue that the enemy spirit world is at least bothered when we worship.

Why would a demon be upset over the playing of Christian music?

The enemy spirit world is bothered by a lot of the things we do. In the inner healing ministry that I am involved in, I hear many who are tormented by demons tell me that when they play praise and worship music, the torment stops. It also stops if they simply utter the name of Jesus. What does this suggest?

I believe we bother the enemy and enable God to do much more of what he wants to do when we line up with him. As I have said above, God seems to have made a rule for himself that he will not work in the human context without a human partner. Starting with Adam to whom God gave authority over the created universe (Gen 1:26–30) and on up through the stories of Old Testament and New Testament saints, we see that God almost always does what he does with the cooperation of human partners. And he even waits for the partners to join him before he acts (e.g., Moses, Jonah).

And it looks like there are things he wants to do that don't get done because there is no one to work with God. In Isaiah 6:8, for example, God is seeking a partner to go for him and Isaiah volunteers to be the one. In 2 Peter 3:9, then, we learn that God doesn't want anyone to perish. But many are perishing. So, God doesn't always get his way, probably because his potential human partners are not cooperating.

God seems to have set things up so that most of what he wants to do depends on his having a human partner to work with Him to get His will done. He is enabled by those who partner with him and apparently limited by a lack of cooperation from potential human partners.

> When we partner with God, he is enabled to defeat the enemy.

When we partner with God, though, he is enabled to carry out his plan to defeat the enemy. Worship is an important way to partner with God. So are prayer, fasting, righteousness, Scripture reading, doing God's will, and anything else that puts us in partnership with God to carry out his purposes.

So, we worship not just for ourselves. We worship for God as well—to enable him to defeat his enemy. A major purpose of worship is not to feed God's ego but to join with him in fighting against the enemy. The same is true of prayer. Worship and prayer are joining God in partnership and the enemy hates them. Worship opens the heavens and banishes enemy spirits. It clears the spiritual air.

I have often wondered about the purpose of prayer (God knows before we ask) and worship (is God an egomaniac?). Neither makes sense if we see the main purpose as either alerting him to our desires or fueling God's ego. But if we see our partnership with God as joining him in his battle against Satan, both worship and prayer make sense. Both are, among other things, acts of war.

Jimmy needs to know that God is at war with Satan and that we are a part of that war. When we worship, the spiritual air is cleansed, the enemy is banished, at least temporarily, and whatever God wants to do is enabled because we partnered with him.

# Hymns Versus Praise Songs:
# Which Shall We Sing

THIS BOOK IS ABOUT communication. We ask, "What do things mean?" The question for this chapter is "What does it mean when we sing in church?" Here are two unsolicited responses to this particular "meaning" question:

A conversation in church between a mother and her young son:

> "Mommy, what are they doing?"
>
> "Why, they're singing, dear."
>
> "Why are they singing to their shoes?"

A comment by a member of my "over 50" Sunday school class:

> "I don't like praise songs—they don't have anything to them. Give me the good old hymns any day. They really say something! [Praise] songs are too repetitive and superficial, more aimed at the emotions than at the mind. They don't treat God with the awe and respect he deserves. They make church seem light rather than serious."

We chuckle at the child's misperception. Yet that is what was getting across to him. And it makes me wonder how many adults get little or no more meaning out of singing from the hymnbook

Why is he singing to his feet?

than that child did. It has become so routine! And how can we worship if we need to spend our time deciphering words written in small print?

The man in my Sunday school class had long "sung to his feet" and felt that was the way it ought to be done. So he was having trouble appreciating the new music we'd begun to sing at our church. His remarks reminded me of the article written by Don Hustad in the Nov. 6, 1987, issue of *Christianity Today* (see appendix A). He was bothered by the fact that we seem to have entered a "post-hymnal age." He sees new generations of Christians losing the riches of the hymnal in favor of repetitious songs so simple they can be easily memorized and sung with an uplifted face and closed eyes to the God we claim to be worshipping.

That's why young people and many of us "oldies" as well find praise songs to be so meaningful. We long ago learned to respect God. Now we are learning to appreciate his nearness. We long ago learned to sing *about* him. Now we are learning to sing *to* him. We've had it "up to here" with information about God such as that presented in most of our hymns. What we need is something to bring us *close* to God.

The Psalmist tells us to praise the Lord *with all of our being* (Ps 103:1). But for generations, almost everything done in church has been a "mind trip." We've learned to worship with our *minds*. The sermons feed our *minds*. The hymns feed our *minds*. The Bible studies feed our *minds*. We have information about God and his works oozing from every pore by now. And we have "informational indigestion" from a lifetime of mind-oriented church experience.

And that's all right—except it's out of balance. There's more to human beings than just minds. Even we "oldies" have emotions And even we (like everyone else) are primarily feeling beings. Like everyone else, *we construct meaning more on the basis of feeling than reason.*[1] We, too, respond more with our hearts than with our heads, especially in those areas

> Almost everything done in church is a mind trip.

1. See my book, *Communication Theory for Christian Witness* (Maryknoll, NY: Orbis, 1991) for more on this subject.

that matter most to us. For us, like everyone else, the distance to our "wills" is shorter through our emotions than through our minds.

We want to be balanced. So we need to catch up in the emotional area. To be balanced in worship, we need to exercise both mind and heart. Hymns feed our mind, praise songs feed our hearts. To worship with only one or the other is to be out of balance.

There was a day when Christians needed lots of information. The pendulum had swung too far in the direction of meaningless tradition. The people needed "content." The hymn writers provided it for them. Charles Wesley has undoubtedly taught more doctrine through his hymns than his brother John ever taught through his sermons. And that's what he aimed to do. That was right for his times.

But it's a different day now. And those of us who have learned to worship with our minds, along with those of us who never learned to worship it all, need something to stimulate us more than we need something to inform us. We need to learn to talk (sing) *to* (God) as praise and worship music does, not just *about* him, as many of the hymns do.

Worship is intended to feed our relationship with God. Who ever heard of friends or lovers who spent their time together simply talking *about* each other? *Talking* about *doesn't feed relationship.* *Talking* to *does.* When we're with him, let's talk (sing) to him.

> We need something to stimulate us more than we need something to inform us.

I love praise music because it helps me worship with that other part of me. It helps me feel and express my love to my Lover. The overload on content with too little repetition that characterizes too many hymns hinders that.

It is interesting, though, that through my love for praise and worship music, I have also come to love hymns more. Through praise music I have learned to sing hymns as I do praise songs—with eyes closed, focusing on the picture being painted by the author's words. This gets my emotions (and my spirit) in gear even when a lot of information is coming at me. And my experience can be complete, because I want to sing both *to* and *about* my Lord.

---

## 7

# Worship: Tradition, or Just "Follow the Leader?"

IF I COULD PLANT one question in the minds of worship leaders, it would be this one: What does what we are doing mean to the participants? Communication specialists tell us that meaning is in *people*, not in the environment or in our words. This being so, the question arises, What do people mean when they engage in what we call worship?

When we were kids, we used to play a game called "follow the leader." There was only one rule to that game: Whatever the leader did, we imitated it. We never asked questions like, What does this mean? or even, Why does our leader do this or that? Our only job was to follow blindly and accurately.

As adults, it's easy to play the same game, especially when what the leader is doing is considered sacred. But the name of the adult game is "tradition." "Follow the leader," we were taught. "It will do you good, and God appreciates your sacrifice." For many, then, the "sacrifice of praise" (Jer 33:11) is a sacrifice of meaningfulness in the name of continuing a tradition.

A tradition gets started simply enough. All it takes is for someone to do something others like and imitate. People start a practice because they find meaning in doing it. Others join in the practice because they, too, find it meaningful. If the practice gets passed on to the next generation, it's a tradition.

The problem is that any given practice seldom means the same thing to the next generation that it did to the one in which it was originated. That is, those who learn the practice from the originators attach different meanings to that practice than the originators had in mind. Our kids (and other followers) may learn our traditions, but we can count on them to attach different meanings to them.

People start a practice because they find meaning in doing it.

How, then, are our worship traditions being understood? Is worship simply a follow-the-leader activity? Or does it really bring people closer to God?

Worship traditions are a part of what is passed from generation to generation and group to group. Worship traditions are learned and followed, sometimes quite passively, by those to whom they are taught. And, since worship is supposed to relate us to God, it is easy for the learners to adopt worship practices for the wrong reasons. Rather than participating in worship because it is meaningful, they may unconsciously regard even meaningless things as sacred in and of themselves.

A worship tradition followed for this reason can be spiritually deadening. Often those simply following a worship leader are not really feeling what they appear to be feeling. They are going through motions originally developed to express praise, devotion, dedication, and the like. But somehow what

Worship traditions are learned and followed, sometimes quite passively.

was intended by the originators has slipped through the cracks, and now it's just tradition.

It's easy to see the deadening effects of the "staid and dignified" tradition of much non-charismatic Christianity. Such groups are in the habit of calling Sunday morning church a "worship service," even though there may be neither worship nor service involved. Even the music (the hymns), intended by those who composed and first used it to express worship, often is no more than transitional between the other components of the meeting. And everything is staid, dignified, and totally unworshipful.

But there can be emotional ritual as well. And much charismatic "worship," though lively, can have just as negative an impact. At the first strum of the guitar, up go the hands, and the faces assume a sublime expression. Emotion is there. But it may mean just as little as the more sedate tradition of other groups.

What to do?

For those who lead worship, Are we leading worship or simply playing "follow me" and making a lot of noise in the process? Worship means exalting our Divine Leader who reads our hearts. If we are merely showing off because we have been given the stage, it is not him whom we are exalting.

A good worship leader creates an event. But events need interpretation. Their meanings are not self-evident. Why we do something is much more important than what we do in worship, as in all of life. The question is not what we do or how we do it, but what it all means. And a little explanation could help a lot.

> Are leaders leading worship or merely showing off?

People do not necessarily get the proper meanings just by imitating the motions. Concentrate not only on the motions of worship but on interpreting and varying them. Don't let potential worshippers simply imitate our tradition. Lead at the meaning level as well as in the forms employed.

For those of us who follow, do we worship when we seem to be worshipping? Or are we simply following a leader? What meanings is our true Leader reading in our hearts?

Worship, whether from the leader's or the followers' perspective, is intended to be more than simply playing "follow the leader." It is to be an excursion into the very throne room of God to see the Lord "high and exalted" (Isa 6:1) and yet with his royal scepter outstretched (Esth 5:2) to us in acceptance, mercy, and love.

To do this, leaders need not necessarily turn completely from their traditions. A little research should be conducted, however, to find out what the traditional practices really mean to the participants. Then some very conscious and well-discussed changes could be experimented with to raise the question of meaning high in people's minds.

Worship is too important to allow the heavy hand of tradition to erode its intended meaning. Give careful attention, then, to the meanings people carry away from worship. Continually ask, What does what we do in worship mean to the participants?

# 8

# Traditions Too Often
# Lose Meaning Over Time

A NUMBER OF YEARS ago, a seminary professor and astute observer of Christian behavior named Delbert Wiens wrote a book titled *New Wineskins for Old Wine* concerning a major problem he saw in his denomination.[2] It seems that the founders of the denomination had come to Christ in marvelous ways out of sinful backgrounds. As a result, all of them could give exciting testimonies concerning the changes their new relationship with Christ was bringing into their lives.

Well and good. Their children, though, were brought up in Christian homes, homes sanctified by the commitment and spiritual growth of parents who knew the difference between a life of sin and life with Christ. But the testimonies of their parents were barely intelligible to this second generation, for their experience had been radically different from that of their parents. Most of these second-generation Christians, however, gave their hearts to Christ early in life and continued in the church. Some even got excited about Christianity. But their children—two generations removed from the experiences of the founders—found much of what they were exposed to in church to be virtually meaningless or, worse, to have negative meanings. So, many of them abandoned the faith.

2. Delbert Wiens, *New Wineskin for Old Wine* (Hillsboro, KS: Mennonite Brethren, 1965).

A major problem in this situation was that the founders of the denomination, like the founders of many denominations, assumed that their own experience was to be the norm for all succeeding generations. They therefore felt that everyone's conversion experience was to involve a dramatic

Children from Christian homes see things differently than first-generation converts.

turning from a life of sin through agonizing repentance to a life in Christ in which everything was new. And they delighted in telling their stories.

But the second and third generations, quite unlike the first generation, had been brought up in Christian homes with the trappings of Christianity all around at home and regular church attendance required. Many of them could think of nothing to repent of when they considered the claims of Christ on their lives. Indeed, they usually decided for Christ at a very early age, before they had had a chance to get into the sins their grandfathers had turned from. So the tradition of repenting from horrible sins and publicly testifying to that fact—a tradition virtually required by the denomination to validate one's conversion—became one of many symbols of irrelevance to the current generation.

## Traditions in the Bible

The same problem happened to Israel. Even the Temple and the Law, traditions that God himself had instituted, had by Jesus' day become symbols of irrelevance, deadness, and even oppression.

*In the New Testament, then, tradition is considered a major enemy.* When Paul calls the Galatians "foolish" because they started in the Spirit but then "turned to the flesh" (Gal 3:3), he is referring to their preference for tradition. Indeed, the whole book of Galatians is addressed to this problem.

The Temple and the Law, once instituted by God, had by Jesus' day become symbols of irrelevance.

Not that tradition is always bad. It is not. But even good traditions can be deadening, especially in the third, fourth, and succeeding generations.

Consider the fact that in most evangelical churches most of the music and worship customs have come from the fairly distant past.

These customs usually sprang from some renewal experience that was very meaningful to those to whom the experience belonged. And the words were those felt most appropriate in that day for expressing what was happening inside them. People were lifted to the heavens when they sang of a "fountain filled with blood" or asked, "Would He devote His sacred head for such a worm as I?" "Guide me, O Thou great Jehovah" or "Just as I am, without one plea" seemed like the right ways for them to express themselves in those days.

In evangelical churches most of the music and worship comes from the fairly distant past.

The organ was the proper instrument to guide the worship for most denominations. And "Thee" and "Thou" were the proper ways to address God. The large, black, leather-bound Bible in antique English and the high, ornate pulpit and robed preacher symbolized the majesty, dignity, and authority of the things said and done during the worship hour. All well, good, and meaningful at one time.

But people are dying spiritually under what seems to many to be the heavy hand of such traditions. *Many churches have moved from conservatism to preservatism.* We have often let our practices become preservers of the remnants of past renewals rather than stimulators of present renewal.

*Real life, however, cannot he preserved.* When I lived in Nigeria, I used to catch snakes, some of them deadly, and drop them into bottles filled with a preservative called formaldehyde. In the bottles, the snakes looked quite real, but they didn't move. They had bodies, but no life. They were preserved.

Many churches have moved from conservatism to peservatism.

Much of church life is like those snakes. There is a body, but no wiggle. The things we do once had life, but no longer.

## What Do I Do about It?

First, look at the tradition. Ask questions concerning where it came from and what needs it met at that time.

For many churches, the tradition hearkens back to a renewal experience that resulted in the founders of a denomination splitting off from another group to be able to express themselves more freely. The tradition in the present may be a formal liturgical tradition; a "semi-formal," mainline, evangelical tradition; or a less-formal, fully emotional tradition. We should ask first, What did it mean to the founders?

Second, ask the contemporary meaning question. What does this tradition mean to the various groups in the congregation today? Some like a liturgical tradition. Why? Some like the "semi-formal" tradition. Why? Some like an emotional tradition. Why? Are the people who prefer these traditions "growing"? Or are they simply "preserving"?

Third, ask which group(s) you are called to appeal to. Some congregations contain representatives of two or all three of these groups (and others). To keep them, you probably will have to alternate between styles and educate everyone about the value of the styles they don't care for.

Other congregations are made up largely of those with a single preference. Fine, unless the preferred tradition is deadening to them.

Fourth, if the present tradition is a preservative tradition, ask what can be done to bring renewal.

> We need to educate people to value styles they don't care for.

One of the interesting things about our society, is that in most of our life we are in favor of change, except in church. In spite of this, however, most people who have changed church type and most churches that have been innovative in worship have found doing so to be renewing. Whether in the Scriptures or in the present day, the introduction of something new has been the common factor in renewal. In Josiah's day, the Book of the Law was discovered (2 Kgs 22–23); in Ezra and Nehemiah's day, it was the rebuilding of the Temple and the Wall; in Jesus' day, it was the newness of His life and message. In each case, renewal accompanied the innovation.

Such things are happening in our day as well. Many people are discovering new aspects of the Christian experience. Healing is one of these. The excitement of witness at home and abroad is another. From such emphases, renewal of worship is flowing in many congregations.

Through changes in worship traditions, many people are discovering a closeness to Jesus they have never experienced before. Some are finding renewal by moving from what I've labeled a semiformal tradition of worship to a more liturgical tradition. Other "semiformal" evangelicals (including myself) are discovering renewal by moving into more emotional traditions. Many of our more emotional Pentecostal brethren, on the other hand, are being renewed by moving into a more "semiformal" tradition. Amazing.

What's the message? Tradition always moves toward deadness as generation succeeds generation. Change, however, can be renewing if it's done right. I'll be discussing such change and what seems to me to be the ways in which it can be brought about in the chapters that follow.

> Tradition always moves toward deadness.

# 9

# Who Do We Sing To?

I'VE BEGUN TO ASK myself an embarrassing question: When I worship, who am I singing to? In the churches in which I grew up, we sang with our eyes open, reading the words in the hymnbook. With hymnbook songs, we were quite sure of what we were singing about, but not always sure who we were singing to. It seemed like we were supposed to sing to those around us. So I learned to follow the notes and sing harmony. And I valued the times when someone sitting in front of me (usually an older woman) would let me know that I had a good voice.

When I became aware of the problem raised by the fact that I was basically singing to impress others, I thought perhaps a more charismatic form of worship would solve the problem. So I visited some charismatic worship services, watched and learned how to worship that way. As I watched, though, I wondered if some of the people in those services weren't having the same problem I was.

For some of them, the first strum of the guitar was all it took for their hands to go up and their bodies to start moving. I asked myself, is this sincere, or simply a "knee jerk" reaction, simply another cultural form of expression, just as subject to being misdirected as the one I grew up with? And the sublime expressions on their faces—are these people really "into it" as much as they seem? Or are at least some of them "playing to the grandstand"?

For some at the first strum of the guitar their hands go up.

Habits like singing to (even performing for) those around die hard, if at all. And they are not simply the problem of one group of Christians. Either hymnbook-oriented or overhead-oriented singing can be reduced to "grandstanding," if we're not careful.

As we worship, we communicate in at least three directions and at several levels—and none of the directions or levels are invalid if used appropriately. We intend to voice honor, praise, and worship to God. So we communicate to God. We do that, however, in the company of others. They hear us, and something is communicated to them as well. Furthermore, we listen to ourselves as we sing. Beyond listening to ourselves, however, we also feel and picture internally, thus communicating within ourselves at levels deeper than words.

By definition, worship and praise music are designed to enable us to communicate Godward. In worship songs we sing *to* God, expressing our relationship with him. In praise songs we sing *about* God and our relationship with him. Sometimes, as we praise and worship, we get caught up in the event and "lose ourselves" in intimacy with God. But what if that doesn't happen? Do we fake it, in an attempt to mislead those around us into thinking we're really "into it?"

> In worship songs we sing to God.

Communicating to others during worship is legitimate. Group worship involves participation. So it is valid to communicate that we are participating, moving together, clapping together, sharing with each other these moments of intimacy with the Father—this is what it's all about. But is this what's really going on? Or are we trying to make others think more is going on between us and God than is actually the case?

Communicating to ourselves is also legitimate. In fact, "intrapersonal" communication is a crucial element in worship. In worship it is good to send messages to ourselves concerning who God is and what we want our relationship with him to be. Just as positive "self-talk" strengthens us in our everyday activities, so such messages directed to ourselves feed and strengthen us in our quest for intimacy with God. As we worship, we remind ourselves of and reinforce various aspects of our commitment to the one we have chosen to be our Lord. Worship "self-talk" is incredibly important.

Furthermore, both older hymns and contemporary praise and worship songs, like Scripture, are rich in images that lend themselves to picturing. As the memory specialists tell us, we record memories in pictures. We can picture the deer longing for water and see ourselves reaching out for intimacy with God. We can picture Jesus shining, the fire blazing, the river flowing, and God's Word going out into all the world. Even older hymns can generate valuable pictures and feelings such as the desire for a thousand languages through which to praise God or singing praises to a holy God early each morning.

But what about the problem we started with, the problem of grandstanding? I find that the more I focus on what's going on internally, the less attention I pay to what I'm communicating to those around me. Closing my eyes helps a lot. So does picturing whatever the songwriter was trying to portray. In order to be able to close my eyes and picture, however, I have to sing from memory. So, whether it's praise songs or hymns, I try to memorize as many as possible.

Like Scripture, worship music is rich in images that lend themselves to picturing.

As I note others around me lost in worship, what they communicate to me strengthens my sense of participation with them in something very important. As I lose myself in communicating with myself about what I want my relationship with Jesus to be, then, I find myself bonding with God more effectively than in any other way.

Worship is too important to let it take us off the tracks by becoming either performance for others or mere ritual. Whatever else we do in church is for now, worship is *forever*. Watch the communicational factors. Line up the self-communication with the God-communication and the other communication will take care of itself.

# 10

# Singing into the Universe

"HE IS LORD, HE is Lord. He is risen from the dead and He is Lord. Every knee shall bow, every tongue confess that Jesus Christ is Lord." We were engaged in delivering a woman from some demons and had decided to sing and worship for awhile in order to weaken them. The demons did not like what we were doing one bit. Why? Two cosmic things were happening: We were making a statement into the universe and the demons were getting weakened.

In a previous chapter I raised the question, "To whom do we sing?" I'd like to come back to that question here but to focus on a different audience. When we declare the lordship of Christ we are, as I mentioned there, declaring that fact to ourselves, to others, and to God. But we are also singing out into the universe to another audience. Cosmic beings are listening. They hear what we say and sing. And they are affected by it.

In several passages in the New Testament it is implied that angels are attentive to what humans are doing (see, for example, Luke 12:8–9; 1 Cor 4:9; 11:10;1 Pet 1:12; Rev 3:5). Indeed, we are told that "all creation" watches expectantly in anticipation of what God is doing with us (Rom 8:19). Some of the celestial beings who are watching and listening are on God's side, some on the side of the enemy.

When we worship, cosmic beings are listening.

I believe they are especially attentive when we worship. The good angels are cheering, the evil ones are not. And our side is helped.

For when we worship, there are spiritual laws that are put into effect. One of these laws is that spiritual beings are enabled to do their jobs better when humans engage in rituals designed to honor them. Every pagan priest or shaman knows this and sees to it that he and his people participate in the proper rituals whenever they seek help from the spirits. Satanists, New Agers, and other occultists know this and give great care to the performance of rituals to honor and worship the spirits they serve. This is what the people of Ephesus were doing when, in order to get rid of Paul, they kept shouting, "Great is Artemis (Diana) of Ephesus!" (Acts 19:28). They were shouting their allegiance to a territorial spirit and thereby turning the balance of spiritual power against the Christians.

In Old Testament days, the empowerment of God's side took place every time the Israelites offered sacrifices, performed rituals, or participated in celebrations to honor God. It happens every time the servants of God are obedient to him. It happens every time we pray, worship, take communion, or otherwise obey or honor our God. This is why praise is referred to as a "sacrifice" in Heb 13:15 and the total offering of ourselves as sacrifices is referred to as "worship" in Rom 12:1.

Novelist Frank Peretti gives an example of how this spiritual law works on the Christian side when in *This Present Darkness* he describes God's angels as waiting to attack the enemy until there is enough prayer (and worship) among the Christians for them to win. When that point was reached, then God's angels attacked and were successful.

God is empowered whenever we obey him.

It is not without reason that God commanded Joshua and his army to take Jericho by honoring him through the ritual of marching, sounding trumpets and shouting (Josh 6). Likewise, with Gideon and his small army (Judg 7).

The effects of ritual, including Christian worship are, therefore, cosmic. Worship involves choosing which side we are on and proclaiming that loyalty to the whole universe. Indeed, worship is warfare.

When we worship we are speaking out into the universe.

It affects more than human emotions and loyalties. It is of great importance both to friends and to enemies in the universe.

When we worship, then, we should be conscious of the fact that we are speaking out into the universe. We are communicating to the enemy and all his hosts which side we are on. We are proclaiming that Jesus is our Lord, not Satan or some human being. We are siding with and enabling the work of the Victorious One to whom every knee will bow. We are aligning ourselves voluntarily and in the present with the "all" who "will openly proclaim that Jesus Christ is Lord, to the glory of God the Father" (Phil 2:10–11).

To worship is to make a cosmic statement. The enemy doesn't like such cosmic statements to be made. That's why he regularly interferes with us as we seek to worship and praise. He knows its power and hears every word we sing. If he doesn't take worship and praise lightly, neither should we. We should never sing "Jesus Christ is Lord" without recognizing the cosmic significance of what we are doing.

# 11

# Some Say Worship
# Isn't Very Important

SATAN IS NOT HAPPY about Christian worship. It really disrupts his operation when people lift their hearts and voices to praise his mortal enemy. Worship empowers the angels to do God's bidding and that's bad news for the satanic kingdom.

So Satan and his followers are on a campaign to keep people from worshipping, if possible. He can keep many people, even many Christians, from going to church. That keeps them from worshipping. But some people just won't stop going to church. And at least some of them when they go to church insist on worshipping. So he needs another strategy.

Let's imagine a discussion between Satan and his followers concerning what to do with those who attend church. The first demon to speak raised the question of just how to keep churchgoers from worshipping. They all agreed that the best thing to do was to get churchgoers to take trips or to get sick so they don't get to church in the first place. But failing that, they needed a strategy for keeping them from really worshipping when they got to church. There were several suggestions. But they clustered into two major strategies.

The first was raised by one of the demons who reported that he had been quite successful in getting families to argue on Sunday mornings before and during their ride to church. He found

One demon got families to argue on Sunday morning before church.

this quite easy since everyone is on the same schedule and, therefore, needs to use the bathroom, get dressed, have breakfast, and even read the paper at the same time. So, he said, getting them into conflict situations was no problem at all. It is especially easy for families with small children. Getting the younger ones to play with their food and the rest of them to argue pretty well assures that they get to church in ugly moods and cannot really worship, even if the church provides good opportunity for worship. Fortunately for us, the demon reported, they did not know enough about their authority to tell me to stop.

Most of the discussion, however, centered around a strategy suggested by Satan himself to get them to believe worship isn't important. If, he said, those who came to church could be made to believe that worship isn't important, we've got them! They mustn't know that their worship enables our enemy to do his work more effectively than otherwise. They must think it is a minor part of what God wants them to do in church and that other things are more important. With this in mind, he and the others made the following points:

1. Newcomers can learn that worship isn't important from the fact that it is the sermon title, not the worship part that is featured on the sign outside the church. This will give them the impression that they can expect a performance by a speaker to be the highlight, with all else as preliminaries.

At that, one of the demons objected that the meeting on Sunday morning is called a "*worship* service." But another pointed out that that's just a name. Nobody who's been going to church for very long takes that seriously. They all know that the main attraction is the sermon. They've been carefully taught that it's THE WORD that's important—presumably the pastor's word since that's what takes up most of the time. So if there's too much time taken up with the singing part, everybody gets antsy because they know the pastor will come on late and go overtime with his message.

2. An important point was made by one of the senior demons concerning what people learn from the status of the church leaders. He pointed out the importance for their cause of the fact that the relative ranking of the things that go on in church focuses on the one who preaches, usually the "senior pas-

Satan loves it when sermonizing is the main attraction and worship is considered secondary.

tor," never on the one who leads worship. The worship leader is always way down the line in terms of status. After the senior pastor come any other pastors and even the youth leaders and last of all the worship leader. This means, he said, that little attention will be given to what the worship leader does.

3. Another demon registered his dismay that the church he was assigned to had recently decided to spend up to half an hour in uninterrupted worship every Sunday. In fact, he said, they even did the message early in the service a few times, reserving the latter part of the time for worship. How he wished they would go back to their earlier format with hymns and songs merely interspersed between the speaking parts of the meeting.

4. One tactic that they all felt a good one was to make sure there is plenty of distraction during worship. We can see to it that instrumentalists (especially drummers) or other leaders get carried away with what they are doing so that people focus more on them than on God. Or that the church leaders are moving around during worship taking care of last minute details. And the more people we can get to keep their eyes open during worship, the more they'll be distracted. Or we can get children to bug their parents and parents to allow them to talk to them or to each other during worship. Or we can see to it that nobody teaches the people the importance of worship or how to do it.

So went the discussion in the court of Satan that day. I wonder if we can learn anything from it.

# 12

## Organs, Guitars, and the Incarnation

"STOP THEM, STOP THEM, stop them!" The voice was that of one of our oldest church members, a woman over ninety years old who could look back on a lifetime of commitment to Christ and to our church. It was the music she was having a problem with. Somebody had brought guitars and (horrors!) a drum into the sanctuary and it was disturbing her.

For this older saint, such modern music could not glorify God. It was the majestic, awe-inspiring chords of the organ (along with a large pulpit, antique "biblical" language, a robed preacher, and stained glass windows) that stirred her soul. Anything "less" disturbed her and, she was sure, disturbed God since, she felt, it robbed him of the honor and majesty due him.

A lot of traditional (mostly older) Christians don't like the fact that the younger generation have become so attached to guitars. Oh, guitars can be allowed for secular things, for play, for frivolity. But why do they insist on bringing guitars into the church? "How far can we let things like this go," the traditionalists ask. "The organ is the proper instrument for worship (and we paid a lot of money for it). God certainly cannot be pleased over a switch to guitars."

There is a problem to be sure. But the underlying issue is not really the music. Rather, buried far below the level of consciousness, is the fact that their whole view of God is under attack. The organ fits that perspective nicely. So do a large, high pulpit, stained glass windows, black-covered Bibles, a preacher in robes reading or praying in archaic language, and a somber choir with soloists who project their voices perfectly but are only partly understandable. All of these things remind one of the awesome, holy, distant, barely approachable God.

Worship for those with this view should be a very serious thing. One is in the presence of God, and all frivolity, all movement, all enjoyment, often much of the intelligibility is to be left outside. God is majestic. We are to admire him, but from a distance. This view of God as distant and unapproachable gets reinforced for older generations and taught to the younger ones constantly through the use of antique vehicles such as organs, pulpits, language, buildings, and the like.

Don't get me wrong. I love organ music. My problem here is not a music problem. It's a *theological problem*. The question is, what impression, what meaning concerning God is received when an organ is played? By contrast, what impression and meaning concerning God is received when a guitar is played? Not that it is wrong to portray the awe-inspiring side of God. Our God is truly awesome

> How do we picture God when an organ is played?

and majestic, "high and exalted" (Isa 6:1). An organ helps us to see him that way.

But if that's all we see we've missed the most impressive part of God, the part that Jesus focused on most. Jesus continually emphasized his connection with us by referring to himself as the Son of Man (meaning "human being"). In becoming a human, he became one of us, uniting God with humanity for eternity. It is this impressive incarnation part that guitars help us with.

Worshipping with guitars portrays a different concept of God. A guitar is a close, uncomplicated instrument. Unlike the organ, a complicated instrument mastered by only a few, a guitar gives the impression that anyone can learn to play it. Furthermore, the player stands on the same level as the audience, not above them in a loft. And the player moves and encourages his/her audience to move as well. Can such an instrument be used to honor God?

Let's look at the Scriptures. John 1:14 says, "So the word of God became a human being and lived among us" (Phillips). An incredible thing, he chose to live *among* us, not high above and distant from us! God's ultimate revelation of himself became touchable—on our same level. Furthermore, he (and the authors of Scripture) used languages notable for their folksiness and intelligibility, not for their elegance. We rejoice in the incarnation, God coming close, uniting with humankind forever.

*Can you imagine Jesus playing an organ?. . . How about a guitar?* God has chosen to come close. It is we who choose to push him away, with music, with pulpits, with stilted translations of Scripture, with preaching styles. Somehow worship with guitars seems to bring him close again. So do praying in ordinary language, pastors who speak personally and come out from behind their pulpits, songs that are joyful, not overly laden with information, and directed *to* God (not just *about* him), and responding with our whole being (not just our minds) to a God who likes to hang out where we are.

> Can you imagine Jesus playing an organ? How about a guitar?

The Lord is here in our midst! How can we be somber? He's come all the way down to our level! How can we be content with worship that pushes him away again? It's a time for expressions of joy. How can we keep from moving? Jesus wants to participate with us. There he is with the guitarists. *It's the theology of incarnation that transforms worship from somberness to pure joy.* Three cheers for guitars (and drums—as long as they're not too loud)! There's important theological truth in the switch from organ to guitar.

# 13

## Organs, Guitars, and Context

WHEN THE PRECEDING CHAPTER was originally published, it engendered some negative responses. Some people are upset that I criticized organs. That's okay. But don't miss the point: God went way out of his way to come close to us. Let's be careful lest the things we do to honor him communicate that he's only a distant God, or only a God of the past.

As I reread the chapter, it became clear to me that I only focus on the organ (or the guitar) for their symbolic value. My critique is of a whole context in which these instruments participate and come to symbolize. What I question is not a matter of whether one likes or dislikes one instrument or the other (as I said, I like organ music). Nor is it about old or new traditions. It is about the unconscious impression that sticks in the receptors' minds, the "communication value" of what goes on when we "do" church.

The items used in a context frequently carry great symbolic value. This means they carry greater communicational impact than normal. For they bring to the minds of the receptors, impressions not derived from the way the item is used in the present activity but on what that item is associated with in other contexts. The association of sitting in pews with sitting as a spectator at, say, musical or athletic events, for example, powerfully communicates that church is a spectator event. The association of organ music with classical, "highbrow" musical events, then, powerfully communicates that church fits into that category. The pulpit is associated with preaching, which, in turn, has strong negative connotations (e.g., "don't preach at me!"). And pastors are known popularly as those who preach and are self-righteous about it.

On the other hand, guitars in popular usage symbolize closeness and contemporariness. Guitars are a part of the contemporary music scene wherever we look. They are in vogue popularly in a way that organs and other more classical instruments are not. It is no insult to organs or organists to recognize that they symbolize distance rather than closeness in our day and age. Personalness and standing "open" to the audience (i.e. without furniture in between), using contemporary language and music and deformalizing the speaking are also symbols of closeness. These are ways of using the context to bring God close to today's audiences.

> Guitars symbolize closeness and contemporariness; organs symbolize distance.

The communication principle at stake is *receptors interpret everything, including the vehicles of communication and what they symbolize as parts of the overall message.* But we are so accustomed to thinking only of verbal communication that we usually ignore the parts of the message that come from the context. The fact is, though, that *much, if not most, of what is communicated in most situations comes not from the words spoken but from the context in which those words occur.*

> These are ways of using the context to bring God close to today's audiences.

To illustrate the influence of context: suppose the Sunday morning worshipper comes into a special place called a "church" that is large, old, communicationally "cold," and filled with people who are largely strangers. He finds his way to a piece of uncomfortable furniture called a "pew," (a kind of furniture and a name that are found virtually nowhere else in his experience). This "pew" is fixed to the floor and arranged with the other pews in rows, so that everyone faces a podium with a strange piece of furniture called a "pulpit" (another fixture and name not used in ordinary life) in the center. This "pulpit" is flanked by seats, piano, and organ (an instrument seldom used outside of church).

Beyond the pulpit are seats facing the audience filled with a choir wearing old-fashioned robes who occasionally sing old-fashioned songs during the meeting. Both their songs and those sung by the audience (called "hymns," another antique word not used outside of church) are accompanied by the organ. In addition, the organist plays something classical (and ancient) before and after the official part of the meeting. The "pastor" (another word used only in this context) wears a robe that is even more antique-looking than those of the choir. He speaks in a formal manner and reads from a Bible translation written in a type of English nobody outside of church uses ... I could go on. But my only reason for mentioning these things is to ask what is the overall unconscious message the participants carry with them when they leave a context like this?

We need to ask questions concerning the communication value of the way we do things.

Beyond the symbolism of the vehicles of communication, however, lies the ways in which the vehicles are *used*. And this gives us some hope. Even in contexts in which the meanings are negatively "stacked," *the vehicles may often be used in such a way that they at least partially compensate for the negative impressions.*

What is the overall unconscious message engendered by a traditional church context?

To underline my point, a few weeks ago, I had two very different kinds of experience in worship services in which an organ was played. The first was a seminary graduation ceremony. The organist is very able and he was playing a very fine instrument. But he apparently could not resist the temptation to show off his skills as he played. This was alright before the ceremony when his assignment was to provide background music while people assembled. It was also okay while the faculty and graduates processed in and out. When, however, we tried to sing the hymns to his accompaniment, it was nearly impossible. He was simply not accompanying. He was playing all over the keyboard as if we who had been invited to sing along with him did not exist.

The following day, however, during the worship service in our church, I had a much different experience, led by a much different use of the organ. Our organist is probably at least as skilled as the one at the graduation ceremony. But he and our music director seem to know the danger of a good organ (or other musical) performance hijacking worship. We sang *with*, not *against*, the organ, and hardly knew it was there because our organist used his talents to *participate, not to show off*. Though our music people can perform and perform well, they use their skills to enhance audience participation. And this usually happens most effectively when they and their skills are least noticed. Earlier in the service we had been led by some guitarists who also used their skills to enhance participation. I have seen guitarists show off and am just as put off by show-off guitarists as by show-off organists.

In a context used by the participants to show off their skills (whether consciously or unconsciously), a major and often overriding part of the message of the way they use their talents is that they are skillful. In a context in which skill is used to enable participation, the major message is participation. In a context such as church where the main activity (including music and speaking) takes place at quite a distance from the audience, a major message is distance.

> We sang *with*, not *against* the organ because our organist used his talents to participate, not to show off.

If the activity is brought closer to the people, closeness is communicated (especially in contrast to the expected distancing). In a context in which nearly everything (e.g., furniture, robes, music, language) speaks of antiqueness, then one of the major messages that gets across is out-of-dateness. If things are done in a relevant, up-to-date manner, however, what gets across is relevance and meaningfulness.

All of these and other aspects of the setting contribute greatly to the meanings the participants carry away from the session. And if the overall impression provided by the context is of irrelevance, antiqueness, spectator event, instrumentalists and others showing off, and the like, it is going to be virtually impossible for the pastor or anyone else to counter those impressions, no matter how relevant his/her message might be.

Suppose, though, that once people get into this antique building, the setting—including seating, podium furniture, dress, music, instruments, the personalness of the pastor, the style of the message, and the vocabulary, both of the speakers and of the Bible translation—are "down to earth" and relevant. The relevant, helpful parts may at least partly counteract the antique parts.

Realistically, we are probably not going to get everything in church changed to do away with all antiqueness. It is even doubtful that such a severing of historical connectedness would be a good idea. We do, however, have to ask theological questions concerning what the communication value may be of the way we do things. I believe strongly that we need to seek to avoid what I call "communicational heresy." Whenever, then, the God who gave his all to get close to us is distanced by the vehicles we use, we are damaging his message. And whenever the participants in activities intended to focus our attention on God hijack those activities so that the focus is primarily on themselves, they are into communicational heresy.

*So, pay attention to the overall context and use it to communicate the right messages.* If this means abandoning an instrument or using it differently, do it. Don't let the verbal message be contradicted by nonverbal, contextual factors.

# 14

## Worship and Relationship

WITH THIS CHAPTER I start a series on communication principles that can be helpful to us in thinking about worship (and many other aspects of life). The first principle has to do with the connection between message content and personal relationship. The principle is:

> Every communication event involves at least two things: the information being communicated and the relationship between the participants. The nature of the interpersonal relationship, then, affects and defines every aspect of the way the participants understand the message(s).

A man dressed in suit and tie is ushered into a spacious office. As he enters, he extends his hand saying, "How are you, Mr. Smith? Thank you for granting me this appointment." Relationship: formal.

A young woman in shorts and tee shirt runs into a similarly dressed young woman on the street. They greet very informally, embrace, and chat for awhile, then decide to go have lunch together. Relationship: informal, close, intimate.

A couple go to a party and unexpectedly encounter a man they dislike intensely. But they greet him politely and even smile and chat awhile so that neither the man nor an observer could detect their real feelings. Relationship: polite, deceitful.

Three relationships: formal, informal, and deceitful. A look at these relationships enables us to predict the nature of the communication that will take place. As these people interact, they will probably use a lot of the same words, especially in the greetings. But the nature of their interactions will not be the same because their relationships are not the same. For it is the relationship more than the words that defines the nature of the communication that goes on between the participants.

Notice this as you observe communicational events. Even with reading, your relationship or lack of relationship with an author will make a big difference in what you experience. A sermon, too, can be quite a different experience if you know the speaker well rather than if he or she is a stranger.

How does the nature of our relationship with God affect our worship? Jesus gave us permission to be on a "first name basis" with him. Not merely formal, and certainly not deceitful but informal, close, intimate.

When we worship in song, what we say to or about God is no more valuable either to us or to God than the relationship on which it is based. We are to worship him from a sincere heart, a heart that is committed to him, loves him, and is obedient to him. Indeed, God wants our hearts to be a part of a self whose every act is an act of worship (Rom 12:1).

> Jesus gave us permission to be on a "first name basis" with him.

Two men were asked to read a passage of Scripture in public. One of them was a great orator, the other a rural pastor. The one read it with oratorical brilliance, the other with feeling and passion. Why, it was asked, did the pastor's reading move the audience more than that of the orator? Because, came the reply, though the orator knew the passage he read and had a formal relationship with God, the pastor knew the author of the passage in quite a different, more intimate and personal way.

Suppose our relationship with God is a fairly formal one. We are in a relationship but not a close one. Our interactions are sort of like, "How do you do, Mr. So-and-so?" "I'm fine, How are you?" And after that we don't have much to say to each other. The nature of our worship will be defined by the nature of our relationship.

Or suppose we are not doing so well in relating to God but we don't want those around us to recognize it. We may even be living in a way we know God disapproves of. Our worship, then, consists of going through the motions basically to deceive our co-worshippers. Our poor relationship with God combines with a deceitful relationship with the other worshippers to completely nullify the value of our pious words.

If, though, our relationship with the Lord is good, the worship we offer will be good. The nature of what we say and do in worship will be defined in terms of the nature of our relationship with the Father. All of the words, the gestures, the music we offer will have deep personal meaning both to us and to God if the relationship is right.

Since God understands our motivations, He will not misinterpret us as another human being might. However, the principle still holds that when relating to God, as in worship, the meaning of what we say and do is pervasively affected by the nature of our relationship with him.

Formal, informal, or deceitful?

# 15

# Source or Receptor Orientation?

THE BASIC ELEMENTS IN any communicational event are the Source (or Communicator), the Message and the Receptors (or Audience). The parts they play in the communication process are as follows: the Source thinks of a Meaning and constructs a Message designed to be interpreted by the hearers as that meaning that he/she then puts into words (or some other form) that are then articulated to the Receptor(s). The Meanings are not passed to the Receptors, only the Message. The Receptors decide what meanings to attach to the message(s) they hear.

Though there are other factors that could be mentioned (for example, feedback and context), the basic elements of every communicational event are brought into focus in this S-M-R picture of communication.

> The meanings are not passed on to the Receptors, only the message is passed on. The Receptor constructs the meanings.

In analyzing a communicational event, including worship events, our first question should be, *What does the Source/Communicator intend (consciously or unconsciously) that the Receptors/ Audience understand by what he/she is saying and doing?*

As we check this out, we may find that the leader(s) suffer from what I'll call a "Source Orientation." This is a very common disease of those who attempt to communicate. It's major characteristic is a primary concern on the part of the leader for what he/

she is doing without much thought given to how his/her activities are being interpreted. Such a Source Orientation is, unfortunately, both very common and often quite unconscious (for preachers as well as for worship leaders).

Many worship leaders fall into Source Orientation quite unconsciously, due to their concern for the quality of their own performance. I have observed worship leaders, vocalists, and instrumentalists whose primary concern seemed to be to impress the audience with their abilities. Such people are fond of doing things that draw attention to themselves. Sometimes, in addition, such people seem to leave us and to move into a world of their own (with their instrument, of course). They may even jump and strut in imitation of the members of secular music groups. Another twist on this Source Orientation is when the worship leader talks a lot between numbers, interrupting the flow of the worship and, whether consciously or unconsciously turns worship into another preaching service.

Many is the time I have had to endure organists and guitarists who insist on using the opportunity they have to show off their abilities. Though these abilities may be considerable, worship leaders are not up there to perform but to lead. Their job is to participate with us in moving into the presence of God, not to hijack the event to parade their abilities. This is quite a different aim than that of secular music groups whose intent is to perform (show off). These secular musicians should not be imitated in church where the aim of the worship leader should be to *participate*, not merely to perform.

Another form of Source Orientation is loudness. Personally, I don't believe God is hard of hearing (nor is Satan). So we don't have to endure broken eardrums to get through to God or to combat Satan. It seems to me that loudness is just another way worship leaders choose to show off.

Worship leaders are not there to perform but to lead us into the presence of God.

A major reason why a Source Orientation is to be avoided is the fact that it is the Receptors who will (consciously or unconsciously) assign the meanings to what the leaders do. Meanings

stimulated by showoff worship leaders, vocalists or instrumentalists are not conducive to the kind of relationship with God we all
want in worship. I know when I'm in an audience led by such
people, I find unworshipful thoughts hard to avoid.

There is, however, another option. That
is to be "Receptor Oriented." Worship leaders, vocalists and instrumentalists with this
orientation continually ask, *What are the*
*Receptors understanding when I'm "doing my*
*thing"?* Am I leading them in such a way that
they are able to bypass me and connect with
God? Or are the things I'm doing intruding
into what I want them to understand so that the attention they
should be giving to God is being diverted to me?

When I'm in an
audience led by a
showoff, I find un-
worshipful thoughts
hard to avoid.

A Receptor Oriented worship leader, vocalist, or instrumen-
talist will make it his/her job to go as unnoticed as possible so that
the worshippers can connect with God with a minimum of interference. Several years ago, while listening to my favorite female
vocalist in our church, it suddenly dawned on me that she has a
fantastic voice. I had listened (usually with tears in my eyes) to
her for years and it had never occurred to me to focus on her singing ability because the messages she sang came through so clearly
that I never noticed her ability. She was, consciously or unconsciously, Receptor Oriented. As I look back I remember she always
chose relevant songs and rendered them in such a way that they
spoke *to* me, not *of* her.

Oh, that all who lead worship could allow the Holy Spirit to
flow through them as effectively as this lady did!

I wonder if it might be helpful both for worship leaders to ask
whether they are Source or Receptor Oriented and for audiences
to be (carefully) polled to see what impressions (meanings) they
attach to the actions of their worship leaders.

# 16

# Information Versus Stimulus

As promised, I am continuing my treatment of the application of communication theory to worship. This time the principle in view is the fact that *every act of communication involves information plus stimulus*. The information or "content" is the part we often refer to as "the message," the part we can write down and remember as statements or pictures. The stimulus part, then, is the part that makes us want to remember or write it down because stimulus is experienced within us. It relates to the need we feel for the information presented at the time it is presented. This is the less tangible element, usually, though not always, signaled by heightened emotions and often definable as impact.

The statement, "John wrote the book of Revelation" contains information that may or may not stimulate emotion within us, depending on whether or not we feel a need for that information. The statement "John wrote the book of Revelation while in exile on the island of Patmos" has a greater chance of stimulating the feeling part of us, especially if phrases such as "in exile" tend to trigger sympathetic reactions within us.

Every act of communication involves information plus stimulus.

Relationships (the subject of chapter 12) can produce stimulus and impact. So can newness. Overfamiliarity and too much content in too short a time can deaden stimulus and impact.

If worship is to be vital, we need both information and stimulus. But, in worship, as in all human experience, there is the tendency for things to get out of balance. For example, the music of the hymnbooks tends to be heavy on information and light on stimulus. Contemporary worship music, on the other hand, seeks to be heavy on stimulus, especially emotional stimulus, and light on information.

We should not choose sides on this issue. For both information and stimulus are needed. Furthermore, for many audiences, an overemphasis on one or the other appears to be God-ordained. For much of church history. as I have mentioned, Christians were "information-poor." That is, they had little understanding of the faith they had supposedly embraced. The Reformers, recognizing this fact, gave themselves to teaching, preaching and singing doctrine. So did the Wesleys. Among other things, this emphasis has provided us with a rich collection of doctrine/information-oriented hymns.

But many of us got what might be called "informational indigestion" from a steady diet of information from the sermons we heard, from the books we read, and from the hymns we sang. We learned doctrine from just about every source we were exposed to. What we lacked was something to get our emotions in gear, something to stimulate parts of us that were ignored as we focused almost exclusively on logically piecing together the bits of information we were receiving.

Then along came the "Jesus people revolution." The kids weren't interested in piling up mountains of information about their new faith. They wanted every part of life, including their relationship with Jesus, quick and loud and bite-sized—fast-foods Christianity. Plenty of stimulus, plenty of action, "two words, four notes, ten minutes."

People with informational indigestion need emotional stimulus.

Off balance? Yes for the young people. But just what us oldies needed to bring some balance to our information-laden worship. So some of us became participants in and advocates of "contemporary worship music" (and raised the average age of the "consumers" of contemporary worship product). We also moved into renewal and greater balance in our own experience between the informational and the stimulus aspects of worship.

But what of the young people? A steady diet of stimulus-oriented materials can break either of two ways. It can simply feed on itself, stimulus producing stimulus, emotional high after emotional high. Or it can create a thirst for more content to bring balance either in the music or in some other part of one's Christian experience. Some have

Young people may need the information we oldies overdosed on.

moved in each direction. And some pastors, recognizing the need this generation has for solid teaching, have sought to provide more information for youthful congregations.

Meanwhile, in churches where the people suffer from informational indigestion, perceptive worship leaders are introducing more contemporary worship songs. And some, at least, are finding it possible to get their congregations "engaged" with (stimulated by) the Spirit to help balance the information-loaded sermons.

And do I detect more content, more information, in some of the worship songs? And can it be that some of the old hymns are being resurrected by perceptive music companies and worship leaders?

Let's be more conscious of our need for both of these elements. Let us, then, strive to communicate the most important messages in the world as effectively as possible, combining useful and accurate information with the proper kinds and amounts of stimulus.

# 17

# Where Is Meaning?

THE PRINCIPLES UNDERLYING COMMUNICATION are easy to miss, probably because we have learned them so unconsciously. Among those that are regularly ignored is the one dealing with the source of meaning. A prominent communication specialist has written:

> Meanings are not in messages . . . *Meanings are in people* . . . Meanings are learned. They are personal . . . We cannot *find* them. They are in *us*, not in messages . . . To the extent that people have similar meanings, they can communicate. If they have no similarities in meaning between them, they cannot communicate.[3]

The principle is, *meanings are constructed or attached to experiences by people on the basis of their subjective interpretations.* Meanings are not *contained* in words, customs, the environment, or any other thing external to people. The object or event does not carry or contain its own meaning. Nor are meanings given to us by dictionaries. Dictionaries merely report the meanings agreed upon by those who speak the language.

*Meaning is a subjective thing*, affected greatly by the associations we make between present experience and past experiences. I once counseled a woman whose experience with her father was so bad that it had poisoned

> Meanings are not contained in words or any other thing external to people.

3. David K. Berlo, *The Process of Communication* (New York: Holt Rinehart & Winston, 1960) 175.

her attitude toward God the *Father*. As with her, our experience with our own father, or with our mother or a dog or a teacher, etc., raises certain thoughts and feelings whenever the word referring to them is uttered. And on the basis of those thoughts, and especially the feelings, we assign meaning to the word.

Such associations greatly affect the impact on the hearers of the words and structures we use in worship and liturgy. The associations in their minds based on their interpretation of past worship experience, lack of experience or even hearsay related to such worship forms provide the material from which they construct the meanings of present worship events.

We may talk about "tastes" in music or art or even in liturgy. Tastes are a form of meaning assigned by people, based on the associations they have with a given item, concept, or event. And obviously taste is something assigned by people, not something inherent in the forms of the music or art or liturgy. We say that "beauty is in the eye of the beholder." So is the meaning of a given approach to worship. This is because appreciation is a meaning, based on learning and assigned by the beholder.

We sort of know this. But we forget a lot, often because the people in our group agree on what is "good" music or art or liturgy and what is "bad." For we learn how to assign meanings in groups. The more similar the cultural conditioning of the members of a group, the more similar will be the meanings they assign to given things and events. People of the same sex, generation, social class, educational level, economic situation, and personal proclivities will tend to interpret similarly.

In worship, then, as in all communication, "the audience is sovereign." That is, the hearers will determine the meaning. Thus, the meaning of what happens in worship is what goes on in the heads of the worshippers, whether or not that is what was intended by the worship leaders. What those who lead worship do, then, needs to be calibrated to the attitudes and preferences of the audience if it is to properly minister to them. For they, the hearers, will decide what

In worship the hearers will determine the meanings.

it all means. And if what goes on is not within the comfort zone of the hearers, the meanings attached are likely to be such that they won't come back.

But there is good news for those of us who seek to bring about change. As mentioned above, the assignment of meaning is something we learn. This being true, things learned can be unlearned. And new things can be learned. And sometimes people are tired of at least certain of the traditions to which they have always assigned the meaning "good." If things are explained properly, then, and by the right persons, they may be ready to go through what is technically called "a paradigm shift" into a new perspective, a new basis for interpreting and assigning meaning to things and events once either unknown or interpreted differently.

This is what has happened to a lot of evangelicals and charismatics who have now embraced a liturgical approach to worship. What was previously unknown to them or even labeled "out of date," has now become an enlivening and renewing experience. Likewise with many traditional evangelicals who have come to prefer "contemporary worship." And there are many Pentecostals who have turned to more traditional evangelicalism for renewal.

People can learn new forms and create new meanings.

Such changes have usually come when people with an often unconscious felt need for something different have met with someone whom they trust to lead them into the new experience. A pastor or other church leader can often be such a "credible witness," helping people to consider new or old things (e.g., music, liturgy) for which they develop new or revised habits of assigning meaning. But things need to be explained. People need to be led, not driven, into changes of perspective on which they can base new understandings and thus new meanings.

# 18

# The Rule that Breaks all Other Rules

THIS SERIES OF STUDIES is highlighting the fact that there are rules by means of which communication takes place and that since worship involves communication, it works according to those rules. The basic rule is that in any communicational event the final meanings are assigned by those who receive the messages, not by the ones who send the messages. Meanings are *not in messages, they are in people. So whatever worship means is up to the worshippers, not up to the worship leader(s) and/or the producers of the music.*

What I want to discuss this time is a corollary to the above rule. But this corollary constitutes a rule that breaks all other rules. It is: *if the receptors are hungry for a given message, it doesn't matter very much how the message is gotten to them.* They will be relatively uncritical of the message and grab it, motivated by their hunger, not by the quality or presentation of the message.

In situations in which one person is trying to convince another of a given point of view, it is important that the setting be pleasant, the presentation logical, and the message attractive to the receptors. If such conditions are not met, the message may well be rejected by the receptors, no matter how reasonable it may be—unless they are hungry for whatever is being presented.

If the receptors are hungry for a message, it doesn't matter how it's gotten to them.

Familiar cases are mass evangelism and Sunday morning preaching. Communication studies show that public communication in which a speaker attempts to convince many people to change their minds is not very effective—unless the people are already hungry for the message being presented. Mass evangelism depends on people coming to the meetings who are hungry. Likewise with preaching. If those who come are not anxious to change, very little change is likely to occur through preaching. On the other hand, messages presented person-to-person in contexts of close friendship very often result in change.

Both mass evangelism and preaching are good vehicles for confirming opinions already held. They are also good at leading people who have already pretty well decided to make a change to make that change. But they are seldom good vehicles for convincing people who are not already nearly convinced—unless there is a hunger for the message, a hunger that has developed prior to the event.

> Evangelism and preaching depend on people being hungry for the message.

But how does this principle relate to worship?

We are all aware of the revolution that has occurred in worship. In the beginnings of what might be called the "Contemporary Worship Movement," it was largely younger people who were attracted by the new forms. There was a felt need, a hunger, on the part of these young people for a Christianity with life in it. "Life," of course, was defined in young people's terms. They were hungry for something alive and different, so they gladly and uncritically turned to guitars and rhythm and overhead projectors and lyrics that sometimes carried weak or even wrong messages—and away from the hymnbooks and organs. For many longtime Christians this seemed like a move away from quality music to a more "worldly" style and a superficial approach to worship. See Hustad's article in appendix A.

It was not long, however, before music companies started to notice that a sizable number of older people had begun to buy their products. And the average age of the "Jesus People" churches began to climb faster than the rate at which the attendees were aging, indicating that older people were responding to the "new" music! The new music was feeding a hunger felt by many older Christians for worship that is more alive, more expressive and less heavy, even if for some the quality of music and lyrics seemed to be sacrificed.

Admittedly, much of this new music, even when the lyrics were unobjectionable, wasn't/isn't strong on content, prompting some of the old guard to bemoan the fact that we seem to be turning away from the "rich heritage" of information-heavy hymns in our hymnbooks. And from a classical point of view, the new music is often not high quality and the lyrics do often seem superficial. But when even older

The new music was feeding a hunger felt by many older Christians.

people are hungry for life, movement, emotion, and songs that can be easily memorized and sung with eyes closed, neither quality of music nor richness of content are the most important things. The rules that favor classical musical taste and old-time, content-full lyrics just don't apply when there is a hunger for closeness to God to be fed, a hunger that wasn't being fed by the hymns.

But the rule that breaks the other rules doesn't work forever.

And there's where a danger lies. Though playing into the "hungry rule" has gained many adherents, both younger and older, we must not forget that the only legitimate hunger in worship is for closeness to God, not for the music itself. And there are many today who are getting tired of the loudness, the showiness, and the trendiness of some contemporary worship experiences where the music itself takes the focus away from the God we are supposedly worshipping.

For many, the hunger for God is no longer being fed and they are back to the normal rules. What are we doing about it?

There are many today who are getting tired of the loudness and the focus on the music rather than on God.

## 19

# Participation Requires Familiarity

I ATTENDED TWO WORSHIP services this week. One was great, the other wasn't. I've been pondering the differences ever since and trying to analyze my own reactions. Since meanings are primarily felt and only secondarily reasoned, I tried to determine first how I felt, then why I felt that way. How I felt: comfortable in one, uncomfortable in the other. Why?

There were similarities. Both worship times were led by gifted and deeply committed worship leaders. Both went for half to three-quarters of an hour and included a number of songs with really meaningful lyrics. The leaders of both events led us in meaningful prayer as well as music. And in both meetings the worshippers seemed to have come there to worship. There seemed to be an air of expectation and devotion that motivated us to participate with all our hearts.

*Meanings are primarily felt and only secondarily reasoned.*

But the differences are the things that stick in my memory and led me to be less than enthusiastic about returning to one of the places. In the event I rate highly, the worship leader seemed to be inviting us to join him as he worshipped. He played his guitar quietly, he spoke quietly, and, most of all, he chose songs that we, his audience, knew, enabling us to participate without having to depend very much on the overhead. Ah, that was it: *participation*.

Personally, I like to worship with my eyes closed. I can in this way shut out what's going on around me and thus fight the self-consciousness and mind wandering that so often intrude into my attempts to worship. When I close my eyes, furthermore, I keep myself aware that worship is a form of prayer and communion with God. So, in that service I was able to commune with God in a most gratifying way. And I continue to have warm feelings as I recall that experience.

Is this a contradiction? Shutting myself off? Communing with God? Is this participation? I think so. Indeed, I *feel* so. Though I shut myself off from the things that intrude, I increased my awareness both of the presence of God and of the fact that this was a group thing.

The other worship service, however, has left me with a kind of emptiness, a memory of expectations unfulfilled. As mentioned, the worship leader was gifted, dedicated, and highly motivated. And she did a good job at leading. But every song was unfamiliar to me! This meant I had to spend much of my time and energy with my eyes open, reading the words on the overhead while trying to master new and sometimes tricky tunes. And it seemed that the rest of the audience was in the same bind, except for a few who seemed to be worshipping without bothering with the words.

Now, I'm in favor of learning new songs. Indeed, with the large number of great new songs that are being produced, it would be a shame if we limited ourselves completely to the old ones. But when the learning load is too great, the ability to worship suffers. Our leader may have chosen the songs she did on the basis of the messages they sought to convey. If so, she chose well. And she may well have considered the potential effect of the tunes on us worshippers. If so, I'd give her high marks for that component.

But the one thing she seems to not have considered wiped out the whole experience for me. That is, *when the learning load is great in participatory events, the ability of the attendees to participate is sharply decreased.*

When the learning load is too great, the ability to worship suffers.

She seems not to have considered the need for familiarity in participation.

There can, of course, be too much familiarity. This can turn participatory events into meaningless rituals. For this reason, it is important to regularly introduce some newness into such events. But this worship leader wasn't even close to that end of the spectrum. One song after another was new.

What should she have done? The worship times I appreciate most start with at least two familiar songs, lead us into no more than one new one before returning to another one or two familiar ones, and may include no more than one more new one before the worship time is over. Such an approach maximizes our ability to participate while also increasing our repertoire. And we can keep our eyes closed most of the time.

> The worship times I appreciate most combine familiar songs with unfamiliar, with most of the songs fitting into the "familiar" category.

An interesting thing to me is that the lesser of these two experiences happened first. I went away from it with the feeling that I hadn't properly worshipped but did not recognize why I felt that way. Not until I had the second experience did I figure out why the first one was so disappointing.

Many worshippers will not have the benefit of such a contrast. They may, however, unconsciously feel let down if there is too much newness. It's up to the worship leader to keep that from happening so they can truly participate.

# 20

# Do We Depend Too Much on Our Worship Leaders?

THE WORSHIP LEADER WAS shouting into the microphone and beating his guitar to death. I was uncomfortable. Was God more likely to make his presence felt if we got louder? It seemed as if the worship leader was trying to generate worship all by himself. Maybe this technique had worked for him last time, or with a different group. Maybe it was just his style and I, as a relative newcomer to enthusiastic worship, was being picky. But it felt as if we were being manipulated.

I grew up in a church where we were regularly warned against the evils of emotionalism. Emotionalism was what the Pentecostals do. They are strange, we were taught, an embarrassment to "real Christians" (i.e., us) because of the superficiality of their understandings and the emotional excesses of their "worship." In fact, we were taught, what they call worship is basically the result of manipulation and emotional hype brought about by their leaders.

We, of course, were largely blind to the considerable amount of manipulation involved in our own unemotional, largely intellectual rituals. It never occurred to us that anti-emotion could be just as manipulative as emotion. Our rituals could be either alive or dead, as meaningful or as manipulative as the "emotionalism" we criticized.

An emotional ritual can be just as deadening as an unemotional one.

But might there be at least a grain of truth in the criticisms of the unemotional? Might emotional worship sometimes be manipulative? I'm afraid so, but for the same reason that anti-emotional worship can be manipulative. For emotionalism, like any other useful technique can be reduced to mere ritual. And an "emotional ritual" can be just as deadening as an unemotional one, and, of course, just as manipulative. But, I'm afraid we often judge both kinds of ritual on the wrong basis. We look at style rather than substance. How do we know what's in the hearts of the participants? It takes two for manipulation to occur—a manipulator and a "manipulatee." Both are accountable to God for what they do.

Back to the loud worship leader. "What are his motives?" I was asking myself. And that little voice within me went on, "Isn't this simply emotional ritual?" "God can't be pleased with this kind of thing." "It looks as though the worship leader is just showing off." "Look at how he tries to manipulate us to get us to some kind of emotional 'high.'" "Is this ethical?"

Some time ago, though, I discovered that I needed to take the initiative in church. For me, as with most Americans, I'm afraid, church had become merely a "spectator sport." I came, I watched, I listened, I critiqued. And I got especially good at the latter, often with what seemed adequate justification. I've been in some pretty poor church services!

But I began to question my own attitude. *Could it be, I asked myself, that my problem with worship is not what they're doing, but what I'm doing?* So I made one of the more important decisions of my whole life. I decided to take the initiative myself to assure that whatever happened up front, or around me, I would meet God. And he and I together would see to it that the experience was an enriching one.

That is, I stopped expecting the leaders to do something for me. And I became a good bit less concerned over their ethicality. You see, when I expect more of them than they can possibly deliver, I am being unethical. When I expect them to do for me what

Whatever the worship leaders are doing, I will worship.

only I and God can do, I am being totally unreasonable. For they are in no way accountable to me. They and I are accountable to the same being. And he alone has the right to judge.

Are the worship leaders trying to manipulate me? Are they simply trying to create something artificial? Perhaps. And that's a very important question for them to get straight with God. But they need to know (and communicate to their audiences) that worship is up to the worshippers. It is the substance of what goes on between them and God that is the point, not the style of the leaders (though the leaders are still responsible before God to do their best to facilitate worship in whatever style is best for any particular audience).

The important question for me, the worshipper is, however, a different one. My question is, Am I going to let their behavior or any other factor rob me of the opportunity of meeting God at this time in this place? No.

# 21

# How Our Worldview Affects
# the Way We Worship

"WE SURE ENJOY WATCHING you when you try to dance," the Nigerian church leaders told me. Enjoy it! They nearly collapsed laughing at me! I was a missionary in northeastern Nigeria and was trying to encourage and identify with their attempt to use traditional music in Christian worship. And it must have been very humorous. My body just didn't work that way. And they wondered why.

In contemporary worship contexts I have a similar problem. "Why can't I lift my hands?" I ask myself. My heart says, "Worship with your body as well as your mind." And those around me seem totally uninhibited. They move, they raise their hands, their faces show total involvement with the music and with the Lord.

But even in that context, I'm self-conscious and struggle to get my hands above my shoulders! "What would my family, my colleagues, those who taught me as I was growing up, think if I gave in to this urge to raise my hands?"

I laugh at myself for being so inhibited. But the problem is a very real one. For buried deep within my psyche are assumptions concerning what is proper and what is improper for a man of my age. We call these assumptions and values "worldview." A worldview consists of all the basic cultural assumptions about how life is to be lived, including how we are to evaluate our and others' behavior. Our behavior, then, is based on our worldview. And worldviews differ from society to society and even from group to group within the same society.

Nigerians have no problem expressing themselves with their bodies as well as their voices. Their worldview not only allows movement, it demands that singing be accompanied by dancing. The same is true, though to a lesser extent, with my charismatic and Pentecostal brethren. But my middle-class, white octogenerian worldview doesn't allow me to be comfortable with such expression of emotion in worship. And I have great difficulty releasing myself from over seventy years of motionlessness!

I've recovered a bit by now. At least some of the time in such worship contexts, I can focus on the Lord, rather than on my own self-consciousness. On occasion, I can even get my hands (usually one at a time) above my shoulders (though only if I close my eyes)! But I still have a worldview problem that I can't seem to simply "will" my way out of.

> I have great difficulty releasing myself from over seventy years of motionlessness.

I deeply appreciate forms of worship other than the ones I've been taught. I love to worship with charismatics, with young people, with blacks, with Hispanics, with "turned on" Chinese and Koreans, with uninhibited Africans—in short, with anyone who moves.

But they have to be patient with me, just as people coming from my background need to learn to be patient with them. For, as an American of my generation, raised in traditional white, middle-class evangelical churches, I have been carefully taught two important worldview values: 1) emotion is bad, and 2) change though acceptable in nearly every other area of life, is suspect in religion.

A major function of religion, according to our Anglo-American worldview, is to preserve past values, not pioneer new ones. My ancestors came from northern Europe. They had conformed Protestantism to their own stolid, unemotional image. They believed that emotion and overt expression of feelings are bad, especially for men. A cardinal rule of behavior is, don't let anyone know how you're feeling. If it feels good or bad, it probably is wrong unless, of course, the feeling is guilt (guilt is a feeling allowed in church).

Adultness and feelings don't mix. "Be a man," I was told as a boy, "don't show your emotions." The worldview assumption is that emotion, feeling, closeness, and bodily expression in general are improper adult behavior, especially for men.

Even Pentecostals learn this and often experience enough uneasiness that they leave their churches and embrace "mainline" worship customs. For, as members of the Anglo segment of American society, we are carefully taught to control our emotions (except at athletic events). And anti-emotionalism gets built into our Christianity as if it were a cardinal doctrine. Church life, then, becomes primarily a matter of "will" surrounded by intellect. We can sing, but don't dare to wiggle.

The second worldview value, then, comes along to set these attitudes in cement within the Christian segment of white middle-class America. In other areas of life, emotion may be tolerated to some extent, at least for women. But in a world that is constantly in flux, religion is expected to give us something firm, foundational, and unchanging, something to hang onto when all else seems to offer no security. So tradition tends to reign supreme in church.

> Anti-emotionalism gets built into our Christianity as if it were a cardinal doctrine.

But there is a ray of hope. There are two other worldview values that are now having an influence in this area. One is the high value we put on youth. Another is the expectation (which we carefully teach) that every new generation will rebel against their parents' generation. Combine these with the fact that large numbers of our youth haven't learned as well as my generation did that emotion is bad and religion is to be conservative, and we have the makings for change.

Some of our young people don't seem to have been taught (as I was) that when we read the Scriptures, we're supposed to ignore the passages where we are told to lift our hands (Ps 134:2) or to dance (Ps 149:3) or to praise God loudly (Ps 150) or to embrace (Acts 20:1), and even kiss (Rom 16:16). And they have often missed the message that it's not okay to change worship styles. So they do these things in church.

And, at least partly because it's okay culturally for adults to imitate young people, some of us adults are getting our worldview changed. Consequently, we're beginning to notice that worship gets defined differently in Scripture. In the Bible, people emoted. They moved. They weren't afraid to express their joy, their closeness, their concern. They danced, they greeted with embraces. Their worldview assumptions allowed them such behavior.

So there's a new wind blowing in America. Many people are more open than they were previously to alternative worship styles. But we need to watch out lest we try to push people too fast. For the influence of worldview values is very strong. Those who attempt to move too fast, therefore, will often be faced with negative reactions sooner or later from those who (usually unconsciously) feel their worldview values threatened.

> In the Bible people weren't afraid to express themselves.

Helping people to appreciate, if not enter into, new styles is the order of the day. People need exposure to and teaching about the validity of new styles. But no one style is right for everyone. Nor will everyone be able to change, even if they enjoy the new style. We may, therefore, need to value and practice patience more than ever before. Those whose styles we see as different, even disagreeable, need our patience. So do those who don't seem to be able to adapt. Each group is valid and deeply loved and appreciated by God.

## 22

# Is the Wiggle in the Drama or
# Is the Stage Shaky?

CHANGE CAN BE A frightening thing, especially to older folks. And, since our society regards religion as an area of conservatism, change in this area can be particularly difficult to handle. With wiggling going on everywhere else in our lives, many of us lock in on our church customs as a refuge from the turmoil around us. So, when somebody tampers with the way we worship, it shakes some people up. They fear that something essential is being sacrificed and replaced by the latest fad.

What they feel can be compared to what an actor or a dancer feels when acting on a shaky stage. Imagine yourself a member of a dancing troupe. You play on many different stages, most of which are quite solid, permitting you to move and jump freely. But, from time to time, you find yourself forced to perform on a temporary stage. As you move, then, the floor under you also moves. And because you fear that something worse may happen, you are not free to perform as you would like.

Or imagine yourself an actor in a play. You know your lines and movements well and feel quite secure in your ability to play your part. You know where you are supposed to stand, what you need to say and do and when to say and do it. But one night you respond to your cue and find that the furniture

> Many of us lock in on our church customs as a refuge from the turmoil around us.

on the stage has been rearranged. Or, worse yet, something major goes wrong with the stage or the props—part of the scenery falls down, a floorboard gives way or sticks up, tripping you, or the braces underneath the stage come loose, allowing the whole stage to sway and shake under you.

Life is like that. The cultural patterns that guide our lives are always changing. The stages on which we act or dance can be quite unsteady. But, we feel, in church we should be able to relax and not have to deal with change.

*Then somebody comes along and changes the worship patterns!* The question then is, is what is happening simply a rearranging of furniture? Or is our previously solid stage getting shaky?

Most people can handle things when the changes are little and not very important—like small rearrangements of furniture in the play. But what happens when a part of the scenery seems to be falling in on us or the whole stage seems to be shaking? What do we do when change seems to be coming too much, too fast? We want to throw ourselves into worship. But every time we move, something under us wiggles that never used to wiggle. So we tense up and can't give it our best.

Is contemporary worship part of the act or of the stage?

The motion of the shaky stage distracts us, breaks our concentration, instills fear within us that something tragic could easily happen. Stages are supposed to be solid. So are cultural patterns, traditions, rituals. They're not supposed to wiggle. Neither are the patterns we follow in Christian life and worship. When change comes too much, too fast, life gets to be like acting on a shaky stage. Everything seems to be wiggling. So people begin to restrict their movements. *People can get very conservative very soon if what they consider to be the stage begins to wiggle.*

Church people often seem like actors on a shaky stage. They seem afraid to move, afraid to act normal, extraordinarily conservative, for fear the stage will collapse. We listen to the parable of the talents and, knowing that the Master commended those who took risks, we imitate the man who refused to risk by burying his talent.

We don't mean to disobey the Master. It's just that things aren't that clear. We want the "stage" of our Christianity to be secure so we can venture out into the drama of life with full concentration on effectively playing our part in that drama. Yet it's easy for us to end up spending most of our time either worrying about the stage or doing our best to repair it (that is, returning it to what it used to be).

But the Christian's stage is both solid and uncomplicated. It is simply, as Paul has said, Jesus Christ (1 Cor 3:11). If our relationship to him is solid, all the rest can be wiggled, especially if the wiggling makes Jesus more meaningful to people. Rearranging furniture or changing costuming or scenery to make the drama more appealing and meaningful to new audiences is all in line with what Jesus did. I believe the Apostle Paul's injunction to become all things to all people (1 Cor 9:22) applies to worship as well as to witness.

Jesus never treated two people or groups the same way. Nor was he in favor of retaining customs that had lost their meaning. There was always newness in Jesus' ministry because the stage of his relationship with the Father was secure. Likewise with the early church. They were always doing something new, trying different approaches to the drama of Christian life. They had one foundation, Jesus Christ (Eph 2:20–22) and "the faith which once and for all God has given to his people" (Jude 3 GNB). There seemed to be no fear of change in Jesus or the early church. *To them, it was the traditionalists, those more attached to the past than related to God, who were the problem.* True Christianity should be oriented more to the present and future than to the past.

But what about those who don't see things this way? God loves even traditionalists, and so should we. So how should we relate to those who seem to mistake furniture rearrangement for stage deterioration?

## Two Principles: Love and Interpret

To love them means to be as patient and considerate with them as you would like them to be with you if you were the one afraid of change. If you like to raise your hands, do you love them enough to allow them not to? If they like hymns but you prefer praise songs, do you love them enough to sing their favorites?

To interpret means to (lovingly) help them to understand that in the kingdom, security is to come from the relationship, not from the traditions, even the worship traditions. Worship traditions need to be constantly replaced for the sake of relevance. People are too precious to allow the drama of an unchanging tradition to mess up the solid stage of their relationship with the Father. For traditions are a part of the drama, not a part of the stage.

Worship needs to be interpreted in love.

People need to be instructed on this subject. There need to be more sermons dealing with the fact that *God wants worship, not sermonizing, to be central in church.* We need to teach that different styles enhance worship for different folks. People need to be taught to look at the looks on the faces of those who respond best to other styles and to applaud and appreciate what those other styles mean to them. God is in favor of diversity and wants his people to stop fearing change. People need to learn that worship style is an exciting variable, not a part of the stage. Love them and teach them this.

# 23

# Expression or Communication?

WHEN I TEACH MY anthropology courses, we try to deal with those things that characterize human life in all or nearly all societies. Art is one of those things. Music is considered an art form. As we study the societies of the world, we find that most people express themselves through a variety of art forms. There are graphic arts such as drawing. There are plastic arts such as carving and sculpting. There are dramatic arts such as dance and drama. There are the arts of storytelling, poetry, and music. Creativity is widely considered to be a major component of our likeness to God (Gen 1:26).

In this area of culture as perhaps in no other, at least certain people demonstrate their ability to create. An important part of that artistic creativity is devoted to self or group *expression*. Through various art forms, whether the carving of sticks, the playing of instruments, or the telling of stories, *people express themselves*, their joys, their pain, their personal inclinations of one kind or another. Most use leisure time to do such things. Some earn all or part of their living in this way.

When people express themselves, however, they *communicate* as well. When someone produces a song, a picture, a drama, or a story, the item produced is looked at and/or listened to by others, creating a communicational situation during which people interpret what is intended by author and performers.

People communicate when they are expressing themselves.

The question is, what is getting across to those who see/hear the artistic expression?

Given that those in the audience interpret from their own backgrounds, what meanings are the audience getting? Are these meanings anywhere near what the originator of the art form intended? And whether or not they are, is what's happening anywhere near what God intends? There are a number of aspects of the interactions between creative expression and the dynamics of communication that affect Christian worship. Though all of these relate to any graphic or plastic art we use as well as to any drama, dance, or other creative expression, we will here focus on music.

1. The original creation of the music we sing usually flowed from a particular renewal experience at a particular period of time. Whether it was to serve the needs of the Wesleyan renewals, those of the Moody/Sankey era, or another more recent or more distant experience, creativity in Christian music has usually sprung from renewal. The vocabulary of that renewal and the contemporary church music style, then, are very prominent in the way the creators of the hymns and choruses expressed themselves.

   The nineteenth and eighteenth-century hymns that fill our hymnbooks were created during a particular time period, sprang out of special sets of circumstances, and feature the vocabulary and musical style of that time. For example, many of those hymns were created, understandably, to focus on the importance to our salvation of the sacrificial death of Jesus. To do this, the authors often used the phrase, "the blood of Christ," a phrase used in older English translations of Scripture to symbolize this central event. "There is a Fountain Filled With Blood," "Are You Washed in the Blood," "There is Power in the Blood," "Redeemed by the Blood of the Lamb," and several other titles featuring this theme have survived to appear in current hymnals. Such words and the musical style of that day

   > Renewals spawn new music.

signified life to those coming into new spiritual experiences at that time.

Without questioning the importance of the truth behind those words, it is doubtful that phrases featuring "Jesus' blood" convey God's truth in our day as effectively as they did a century ago to those Christians, not to mention to contemporary non-Christians. I have observed Christians using the phrase as if it was magical. To others, it simply is another indication of the out-of-dateness and irrelevance of what we do in church. For, if the messages communicated by last century's authors are to get across today, the words and musical forms will have to be just as appropriate to today as those were to their day. If not, their meanings will be changed. A basic principle of communication is that the cultural forms of one time period will not convey the same meanings in another. If, therefore, we want to communicate the same message today, today's forms need to be used.

2. A second, and quite different aspect of the interaction between expression and communication, is the question, when a singer sings, is she or he primarily attempting to communicate the message embodied in the words? Or is the singer mostly just showing off? A musical piece is initially the expression of the author. But those who perform it get to express messages through it also. Many performers, then, take the opportunity to change the message the author intended to a message like, "See how talented I am" or at least to let such a message intrude into the message of the words. When this happens, the performers create a different communication focus than was intended and the message gets changed.

The cultural forms of one time period will not convey the same meanings in another time period.

*Communication is most effective when the vehicles of that communication, whether persons, words, music, or whatever are not noticed.* When, therefore, our attention is attracted to the talent (or lack of talent) of the performer, the message of the author is obscured and replaced by the intended or unintended message of the performer.

3. A third aspect of this interaction to watch is that of the expectations of the audience. We live in a society in which we do a lot of spectating. We watch a lot of performances, whether these be dramatic, athletic, musical, or oratorical. We have, then, the habit of entering a place filled with seats with a platform at the front and settling back in our seats to watch a performance. This means that our tendency will be to treat church as a series of performances. There are prayer performances, music performances, announcement performances, a sermon performance and the payment for the performances via the offering.

Communication is most effective when the vehicles are not noticed.

When we watch secular performances, we evaluate them. It was a good or a poor drama, athletic event, speech or musical presentation. This habit affects us, then, in church. As we leave church, we want to let the performers, the pastor, the musicians and any others, know they performed well. Now, any time anyone stands up in front to communicate anything, there will be a performance. Whether or not the person performs is not the question. Nor even whether or not he or she performs well. The question is, what is communicated?

Poor performers, egotistical performers, and those with an accent draw attention to themselves, away from the message they were supposed to convey. But even those who do their best to keep out of the way of the message often bump into this problem of the expectations of the audience. The principle is *the expectations of those who receive communication color every aspect of the messages they receive*. I believe our church people need some help with these problems.

Audiences can be helped when those in front recognize and do something about what's going on. One of the most helpful things I've heard is when a musician (whether vocal or instrumental) invites the audience to close their eyes to try to picture what the song is about. This kind of assistance helps both performer and audience to counter the temptation to fall into undesirable habits, whether of showing off or of expecting an entertaining performance. Often, simply

To enhance the experience we can close our eyes to picture what a performer is trying to communicate.

explaining the problem is enough to help us to transcend it. Older hymns can often be sung with much more meaning if the context and the antique wording are simply explained. It could be helpful, in addition, to sing a more contemporary song with a similar meaning back-to-back with the older hymn.

A major problem with communication is that so much of it is subsurface. Often, the best remedy is to bring the problem to consciousness, first the consciousness of the leaders, then that of the audiences. People can learn to use and interpret music and other art forms differently. I remember how cheated I felt when a creative dance was done in our church but we were not told how to interpret it. I could simply admire the movements of the performers. I didn't understand what they were trying to get across because I hadn't been taught the code.

Let's not leave people hanging or unconsciously overpowered by habits learned in other settings.

---

## 24

# Worship and Church Growth

I WAS ASKED TO preach at a church in Pittsburgh several years ago. Before it was my turn to speak, I participated with the congregation in one of the most inspiring worship experiences I have ever had. The worship was simple but moving, quiet and centering our thoughts on Jesus, contemporary and anointed. It was clear to me why that church has been growing rapidly over the past several years (from five families to nearly 2,000 members in thirteen years). It is one of an increasing number of "post-denominational" churches that combine contemporary worship with evangelical preaching and a balanced, low emotion practice of the gifts of the Holy Spirit.

Everything in human life needs to be analyzed in terms of two closely interrelated realities: the human and the spiritual. And there are rules governing how the human and the spirit-world interact. One of these is that obedience at the human level enables God to do his will "on earth as it is in heaven" (Matt 6:10) if, in addition, the forms used at the human level are attractive to people a powerful draw is created. When people are attracted to worship and in the right place spiritually, the Holy Spirit breaks through the spiritual barriers and the church grows for the right reasons. When, however, there is sin, wrong motivation, and/or other forms of disobedience, though the church may grow, the bond between God and the worshippers that enables the Holy Spirit to do his work is weakened or non-existent.

Though there are many in the churches who prefer traditional to contemporary worship, most of the rapidly growing churches in America are into contemporary styles somewhat like that of this Pittsburgh church. In such churches, many are learning what real worship is for the first time. And many outsiders are being attracted to a Christianity that seems to them to be up-to-date.

There is activity in the spirit world paralleling the activity in the human world.

But growth needs to be looked at carefully. We cannot simply take it for granted that all church growth is for the right reasons. Not all that is contemporary and attractive is from God—even if it results in church growth. Not all that attracts people to a church can be considered biblically appropriate. Questions need to be asked concerning what is happening at both human and spirit-world levels. Are people attracted simply because this music is more like what they hear out in the world, giving them an emotional "high"? Are the worship leaders in the right place spiritually or simply putting on an attractive show? For leaders and people alike, is there enough human obedience for God to be working?

The enemy has much to gain by interfering with worship. I have experienced contemporary "worship" that is too loud, or too centered on one or more performers, and this in churches that are growing. Such churches attract those for whom going to church is a spectator sport where one attends primarily to enjoy the performance put on by musicians and/or pastor. These churches communicate

The enemy has much to gain by interfering with worship.

relevance and, therefore, may grow, but for wrong reasons.

We need to ask, When people come to church, do they really connect with God? Or are they simply experiencing the meeting of other felt needs? With the large population we have in America, it is possible for just about any attractive group experience to draw an audience. Though we may communicate relevance, are we really enhancing the crucial relationship with God that is the all-important end of worship? Even if there is good growth, and reasonably good worship, we need to constantly monitor what we are doing lest we drift into something less than what God desires.

What does worship have to do with church growth? Worship that fulfills both human and divine criteria enhances the growth of God's groups both qualitatively and quantitatively. It communicates the presence of God. People are made for closeness to God. Even non-Christians thirst for such closeness, though they may not be conscious of it. Solid, sensible, meaningful worship attracts the thirsty. So does the power of the Holy Spirit that flows through the worship forms. A church that regularly leads people into closeness to God through worship, deserves to grow, both for spiritual and for human reasons.

There are many factors to discuss when analyzing church growth. Worship is one of the most important. It is important and attractive to be contemporary. That fulfills the human component of the equation. It is also important that leaders and people alike be as spiritually "clean" as possible. With both spiritual and human criteria met, then, we must always work through worship to bring about growth in relationship with God. Good communication involves both content and

Worship that fulfills both human and divine criteria enhances the growth of churches.

relationship. Whatever the content of the worship vehicles and all else that goes on in church, it is the relationship with God that will determine the value of that content—and the quality of the growth.

## 25

# Media Are to Serve, Not to Be Served

A GENERATION AGO, MARSHALL McLuhan caught the public eye with his famous overstatement, "The medium is the message" (or the "massage"). What he meant was that when those who receive messages assign meanings, *they interpret the medium as an important part of the overall message.*

If, then, people feel good about the medium through which the message comes, that medium will contribute positively to the meaning. "Soft" music, for example, is felt by most to be appropriate to worship and, therefore, enhances worship when combined with appropriate lyrics. If, however, the participants feel there is some incompatibility between the message and the medium, the result will be a negative input into the meaning.

People interpret the medium as a part of the overall message.

For many, the medium of loud rock music is incompatible with Christian lyrics. The result, therefore, is negative no matter how uplifting the words may be.

If for some reason the medium is confusing, that confusion enters into the interpretation of the message by the receptor. Though one can admire the technical expertise of the fifty visual bytes per minute of the MTV style, the overall impact for most may well be confusion rather than effective communication. I have seen several attempts to use that style in church contexts and have not yet found anyone who considered it helpful. To the extent that such a style is confusing to any given observer, then, to that extent it hijacks the meanings conveyed.

We are in an age of incredible innovation in media technology. And the church needs to keep current in this area. Whether in the keeping of records or the networking with other ministries, there is much help to be gained on the organizational side from the use of new media. As long as the issue is the processing, passing on or storing of information, computer technology can be very helpful.

There is, however, the danger that we will get so fascinated by the usefulness of technology in handling information that we begin to use it in more public areas to which it is not so well suited. We may, in fact, find ourselves sacrificing both time, energy, and some important aspects of the essence of our messages in our attempts to be "up to date." I have on occasion interacted with Christian media people who are so sold on their particular media that they ignore the fact that the expense, time expended, and minimal communication value of their product (not to mention the confusion experienced by many) are counterproductive to the ends they are supposed to serve.

In Christian communication, we have a major problem in relation to most types of media. This problem relates to the nature of our message. As I pointed out in my book *Communication Theory for Christian Witness*, Christian messages are "person messages," not simply "word messages" and *the only totally appropriate media for these messages are human beings.*

A typical word message involves merely the passing on of information, as in a news broadcast. Newscasters, though they project some personality as they read the news, are not required to get involved in the messages they read. What their personal lives may be is irrelevant to the messages they present. Christian messages, however, require personal involvement. They are messages rooted in life for the purpose of creating and cultivating person-to-person relationships. When, then, in preaching, teaching, writing

Christian messages are person messages, not simply word messages. They come in life, not merely in words.

or electronic media we reduce Christian messages to mere words or flashing pictures, we do injustice to the message.

The only totally appropriate medium for person messages is persons. Christian messages have to be life-related in a profound way if they are to accurately put across what God intended. But the hopeful thing for the use of media is that if done rightly, media can be used to convey person messages. The Bible, for example, is in written form. Even in writing, though, it is person-centered, conveying its messages in a way that invites contemporary readers to identify with the characters in a personal way and to be involved in the same kinds of growth and transformation recorded there. The communicative value and power of the Scriptures lies, humanly speaking, in the fact that they are a record of person-to-person interactions designed to produce in us similarly personal reactions and events. The Scriptures thus illustrate that even person messages can be presented through an impersonal medium such as writing if the use of the medium is properly fit to the message.

Unfortunately, sermon after sermon, book after book, radio or TV broadcast after radio or TV broadcast, PowerPoint presentation after PowerPoint presentation have regularly been used in such a way as to *reduce* relationship-oriented person messages to information-oriented word messages. Our relationship-oriented God is thus reduced to a God of information, doctrine, and perhaps to glitzy visual presentations and relationship-oriented worship to ritual or fascinating but communicationally detrimental special effects.

> The Bible is a casebook of personal interactions relating to God.

None of this in and of itself does away with the possibility of using current technology. Indeed, there are many ways in which audio and video media can enhance the "personness" of our messages. It is refreshing, for example, to see the deadening word-orientation of most sermonizing supplemented by drama, video, person-oriented worship, and even the judicious use of Power-Point or even overhead projectors as enhancers of teaching. The criterion we must use, however, is whether or not the technology contributes to the personness of the messages. An additional thing to look at, then, is whether the amount of time expended producing the special effects is really worth it. God's love affair with humans is too exciting and transformational to be sacrificed on the altar of technological up-to-dateness.

So, go for the technology. But be principled about it. Use it for all it's worth. That's why God gives it to us. But don't be subject to it. *A person message demands a person medium.* When technology intrudes into the personness of our messages, it hijacks the meanings and reduces them to less than Jesus gave his life for.

# Appendix A

## Let's Not *Just* Praise the Lord

*What is the proper place of those
popular praise and worship songs?*

Donald P. Hustad [1]

[From *Christianity Today*,
November 6, 1987, pages 28-31]

ARE WE ENTERING A "post-hymnal" age? As strange as it may seem, the answer for now appears to be a qualified yes.

It was Martin Luther who capitalized on the development of print and gave the German people the Bible and the hymnal in their own language. And it was this that allowed Reformation believers to hear God through his Word and speak to him through the hymnbook. Today, however, the hymnbook is being increasingly discarded as part of the church's accommodation to the video revolution.

Many church leaders say traditional hymns are too hard to understand, too theological in language. Some have discarded their hymnals in favor of simple worship choruses sung from memory

1. Dr. Hustad's family grants permission to reprint this article. Dr. Hustad continued to address this and related matters of worship and culture until his recent death. His thoughts may be explored in Jubilate II: Church Music in Worship and Renewal (Hope, 1993) and True Worship: Reclaiming the Wonder and Majesty (Hope Publishing Company and Harold Shaw Publishers, 1998).

or with the help of an overhead projector. But these uncomplicated songs may in fact mirror the video age in which they were born: as short and encapsulated as news stories, and as repetitive as fast-food commercials.

Let us take a closer look at these "tiny hymns"—miniature both in length and in content—that threaten to replace our historic hymns. Their very title— "praise and worship" music—suggests they are principally texts of adoration and praise. This is surely commendable—despite their obvious limitations—and we should be grateful the movement has revived the ancient practice of singing Scripture verbatim. But labeling this new form suggests "praise and worship" texts are new, and that is surely not true—our hymnals are full of worthy "praise and worship" word. These new pieces are short, often no longer than two lines. Their main characteristic is simplicity; usually only one idea is stated, and it may be repeated many times. Those having more than one "stanza" change only a word or two with each repetition. Nor is the music really contemporary in style. With a few exceptions (mostly borrowed from Jewish folk dances), the tunes and harmonies are ultrasimple in the gospel-song tradition.

Perhaps the best illustration of this is the popular chorus "Alleluia." It repeats that word of praise eight times, using only four different melody notes and three chords. The second stanza repeats the words "He's my Savior" eight times, with similar changes in the third, fourth, and fifth stanzas.

Before it appeared in print, the chorus was learned in a much stronger oral tradition. In it the words "He's my Savior" of the second stanza were alternated with the word "Alleluia," and so on. This version gave each stanza both unity and variety—an agreed norm for both a work of art and a folk hymn with its own artless charm. But then, it would not then be so simple—and today, simplicity is in!

## Nothing New Under the Sun

But choruses are not new. They are the logical successors of the refrains of gospel songs and the "spirituals" (of both black and white heritage) that emerged from the camp-meeting revivals of the early 1800s. Furthermore, *those* well-known forms were patterned after the alternation of stanza and refrain that has always characterized secular folksong. A refrain would contain or suggest the central message of a song; then it was interspersed with stanzas elaborating on that theme.

In nineteenth-century revivalism, the refrains or "choruses" of gospel songs were often sung without using the stanzas. Simple songs—like "Draw Me Nearer," "At the Cross," "We're Marching to Zion"— became even simpler: only the central thought was expressed. And they could be sung spontaneously, from memory.

So, who needs a hymnal?

The next logical step was to omit the stanzas completely, and simply write the refrain, or "chorus." This was common in the 1940s in the Youth for Christ (YFC) movement. Choruses were standard fare in the Saturday night mix of worship, evangelism, and entertainment. But those choruses were quite different from today's. They usually expressed the same concepts as their gospel song antecedents—narratives of Christian experience or devotional expressions directed to Jesus alone. Typical of these choruses are "Gone, gone, gone, gone! Yes, my sins are gone"; "I have the joy, joy, joy, joy, down in my heart"; "For God so loved the world"; and "Every day with Jesus is sweeter than the day before."

These earlier forms were all products of renewal movements in the church— first in the highly emotional brush-arbor camp meetings of the early nineteenth century; later in the urban-centered "Second Awakening" under Charles G. Finney and the evangelistic efforts of D. L. Moody, R. A. Torrey, and Billy Sunday; and finally in the parachurch movements associated with Youth for Christ and radio evangelism. It should not be surprising that the new choruses first appeared as part of today's charismatic renewal movement.

It may be argued that these new expressions are stronger than the YFC choruses, since they express adoration and praise rather than personal testimony. "King of kings and Lord of Lords, glory hallelujah," "We have come into his house and gathered in his name to worship him," "Don't you know it's time to praise the Lord," "I love you, Lord, and I lift my voice," and "Sing hallelujah to the Lord" are good examples. Many of these texts abound in Scripture quotations, especially the Psalms. Some, like "Worthy is the Lamb that was slain," "Bless the Lord, O my soul," "Thou art worthy, O Lord," "I will sing of the mercies of the Lord," and "Seek ye first the kingdom of God," are taken completely from the Scripture.

## Praising Praise, Worshiping Worship

Take just one of these refrains and compare it with the worship hymns it maybe replacing. For instance, "Let's just praise the Lord" seems to express a casual approach to the holy service of worship. The problem may be with the word *just*—as in "Let's *just* sit down and have a cup of coffee."

The following exercise might be more revealing if the words were spoken audibly, which the reader may or may not choose to do:

> *Let's just praise the Lord!*
> Praise to the Lord the Almighty, the King of Creation!
> O my soul, praise him, for he is your health and salvation!
> *Let's just praise the Lord!*
> A mighty fortress is our God, a bulwark never failing,
> Our helper he, amid the flood of mortal ills prevailing.
> *Let's just praise the Lord!*
> Holy, holy, holy, merciful and mighty,
> God in three persons, blessed Trinity!
> *Let's just praise the Lord!*
> Immortal, invisible, God only wise,
> In light inaccessible hid from our eyes.
> *Let's just praise the Lord!*
> O worship the king, all glorious above,
> O gratefully sing his power and his love.
> *Let's just praise the Lord!*
> Great is thy faithfulness, O God my Father,
> There is no shadow of turning with Thee.

The constant repetition of phrases such as "Let's just praise," or "Come, let us worship the King," or "Don't you know it's time to praise the Lord" sounds more like an "invitation to praise" than praise itself. An Assemblies of God leader from India recently said his American friends seem to be "praising praise" and "worshiping worship." But the larger hymns not only call us to adoration; they describe the excellence of God and recount his promises and mighty deeds—stating the motivation for worship.

## The New Testament Standard

Some Christians prefer to be called "restorationist" because they believe they are returning to the worship and ministry experiences of the apostolic period. But how closely do they follow the early church's standards for worship music?

The apostle Paul mentions three distinct types of song: "psalms and hymns and spiritual songs" (Eph. 5:19, Col. 3:16). We believe these were different types of music—in origin, in text, and possibly even in the way they were performed.

*Psalms* no doubt included all the psalms and canticles common to Jewish worship—the historic, classical worship expressions known to all Jewish Christians who had grown up hearing them in the temple and the synagogue: songs of praise and thanksgiving to Yahweh, didactic psalms, witness psalms, psalms of petition and lament.

*Hymns* were probably new songs that expressed the Christology of the new sect. A number of these hymns appear in Paul's letters, written in the patterns of classical Greek poetry. Like many of the hymns of Martin Luther and Charles Wesley, they were written to express, and thus teach, Christian doctrine. One is in the form of a simple creed, or statement of faith:

> Great indeed, we confess, is the mystery of our religion:
> He was manifested in the flesh, vindicated in the Spirit,
> seen by angels, preached among the nations, believed on in
> the world, taken up in glory.

(1 Tim. 3:16)

In another example, the poetic (and possibly antiphonal) form is obvious:

> The saying is sure:
> If we have died with him, we shall also live with him;
> if we endure, we shall also reign with him;
> if we deny him, he also will deny us;
> if we are faithless, he remains faithful—for he cannot deny himself.

(2 Tim. 2:11-13)

The patristic fathers and modern musicologists both agree that *spiritual songs* described ecstatic singing that was either wordless or had unintelligible words—singing in tongues. It is the one type of New Testament song that belongs exclusively to modern-day Pentecostals and charismatics. But it is still fair to ask: How does the new music measure up to the total spectrum of New Testament musical practice?

The new chorus literature is—according to its title—exclusively "praise and worship." But many would contend that if this is the church's only song, praise becomes both simple and simplistic. On the one hand, we ought to rejoice that the movement has reinstated the practice of singing the words of Scripture. But Scripture choruses are but snippets of Holy Writ; their use may be compared to singing "proof texts." On the other hand, Roman Catholics, by comparison, today sing or say major portions of a psalm in every celebration of the mass. Over three years, in just Sunday observances, over 150 different psalm passages will be used. Furthermore, modern choruses pointedly omit all the expressions of the didactic, the penitential, and the petitionary psalms, and contain nothing comparable to the psalms of lament. Nor does the new music make an effort to teach the doctrines of our faith.

Moreover, except for the Scripture fragments used, this type of contemporary worship tends to ignore the traditional forms that express the continuity of our faith and the perpetuity of God's covenants with his people. The early Christians knew they were still the children of Abraham, Isaac, and Jacob—but also of David and Solomon and the prophets who left their songs to be sung in worship. The sixteenth-century followers of Luther understood that they had the same heritage, and they added the patristic and medieval hymns of Ambrose of Milan, Fortunatus, Gregory the Great, Francis of Assisi, Rhabarius Maurus, and of the two Bernards—one of Clairvaux and one of Cluny.

Until recently, evangelicals acknowledged in their music their identity with the same family tree, and we added the hymns of Luther, Gerhardt, Calvin, Wesley, Newton, Bonar, and many others. When we stood to sing their songs, we were joining our own spirits and voices with theirs and the thousands of believers who followed in their train, exulting in the glory and redeeming love of God. And our faith was strengthened. Today, some of our family of faith seem to be willing, even eager, to discard this heritage for a simpler fare that may disappear as suddenly as it has flowered.

It is probably true—especially in our less-literate day—that many worshipers have difficulty finding their way through the phrases of a standard hymn. But should we reduce our liturgical statements to those that every person, of any age, will understand immediately? The answer, of course, is no. Like the ancient creeds of the church, like many passages in Scripture—like even the Lord's Prayer—we repeat them because the historic and continuing church has found in them its understanding of our faith. Their meaning comes to us slowly, but surely. And in the meantime, their truth has been preserved for us and for our children. It is still true, as C. H. Sisson said, and Brian Morris quoted in *Ritual Murder:* "There is no such thing as passing on profound truths in superficial speech."

*We cannot expect this generation to respond*
*to hymns that are rich in content unless they are taught*
*carefully and used convincingly.*

## Using the New Music Well

An increasing number of church musicians admit they have reluctantly added this music style to their worship resources. They felt compelled to do so by the large number of folk who heard "praise and worship" music in another "successful and rapidly growing" church, and came home with glowing reports of its significance. Competition, after all, is a factor in church life today: If you don't give people church music they want, they may go down the street where they can get it.

In a recent article, "What to Do with Church Hoppers," William Self, pastor of Wieuca Road Baptist Church in Atlanta, said: "I've been hammering my folks with the need to be steadfast, unmoveable, always abounding in the work of the Lord—not a popular theme in these days of rootlessness. Somehow, we have to make disciples instead of inspiration junkies."

Disciples, of course, are people accustomed to discipline. And how many of our folk understand that the central requirement of worship is not "getting a blessing," but giving God an acceptable sacrifice of praise? A true sacrifice is always a costly thing, not a demand for instant gratification of our pleasure needs.

Even so, it may be wise to use the best examples of the new music. It is surely an appealing form in our day and probably an example of the folkish styles that tend to appear in times of spiritual renewal. The "tiny hymns" are quite ideal for an informal service in the home or on the beach, for Sunday evening worship or the prayer meeting. In regular worship, these choruses can be used much like the historic antiphons, preceding and following a more serious, more didactic hymn.

For instance, "Let's Just Praise the Lord" could provide an introduction and coda to the chorale to which we compared it— "Praise to the Lord, the Almighty." The chorus "He Is Lord" would help prepare the congregation for the biblically based, theologically rich hymn by F. Bland Tucker, "All praise to thee, for thou, o King divine, didst yield the glory that of right was thine, that in our darkened hearts thy grace might shine. Alleluia!" Others would serve well as preparation for, or a response to, the pastoral prayer.

Some churches are using this music as "preparation for worship." In our evangelical tradition, the organ prelude is, unfortunately, not used as an aid to quiet meditation, serving merely as background—even as competition—to the noisy "fellowship" that seems to be the first priority for many. So in some churches, these "tiny hymns" are sung for about ten minutes before the service begins. As a result, conversation ceases and there is opportunity for a gradual quieting of the spirit and focusing of the mind in preparation for the meeting with God. When the service begins, using the standard hymns of the church in good liturgical design helps to make their meaning clear.

## Must Our Worship be Nonliterate?

We cannot expect this generation to respond to hymns that are rich in content unless they are taught carefully and used convincingly. The shallow-but-pleasurable emotional response to worship choruses is derived from the repetition of a few simple phrases. Those who expect worship to be more reasoned and rational must patiently and lovingly introduce their people to the deeper emotional resources of *words* that will truly challenge and stimulate the imagination. Texts of great hymns have done this since the sixteenth century, and they still have the power to do so—even in this post-Gutenberg era. Perhaps we can use our new nonverbal languages to clarify the meaning of words, and vice versa.

It may also be argued that the younger generation is "turned off" by certain classic hymns that contain obscure and/or archaic language. Hymnal editors are encouraged to revise the texts of older hymns to match the new Scripture versions and modern prayer language, so that God is addressed as "you" instead of "thou." Many churches would also insist on the elimination of sexist language pertaining to people; for example, "Good Christian Men, Rejoice" is easily changed to "Good Christians All, Rejoice."

Church musicians and ministers should also get to know the rich new hymns being produced today. It is ironic that many churches overemphasize ephemeral, simplistic materials and ignore the "explosion" of exciting new hymns being produced in Great Britain and North America by Timothy Dudley-Smith, Bryan Jeffrey Leech, Margaret Clarkson, Fred Pratt Green, Bryan Wren, Christopher Idle, and others.

## Turn off the TV!

A recent public-service announcement aired on NBC Television offers some sound advice. In it, Steve Allen, the gifted musician and comedian, appears and says: "Don't let television dominate your life. Walk over and turn the . . . thing off. Get a good book and read it!" Perhaps, for us, that book might be a hymnal, a stimulus to aid our personal worship.

This practice was common in earlier times, when worshipers carried the hymnbook, as well as the Bible, to church. At home it was used for singing in family worship and for reading in personal devotions.

A good hymnal contains many paraphrases of Scripture and is a compact handbook of Christian theology in poetic form. It also includes noble examples of all the forms of prayer with which we *respond* to God's self-revealing—adoration, confession, thanksgiving, petition, supplication, surrender, and dedication. It can supply thoughts and words to express our devotion when we have difficulty finding our own. Used regularly, it enlarges and enriches our personal vocabulary of worship, and—when we meet in church on Sunday—helps us sing the hymns with joy and understanding.

*The late Donald P. Hustad was senior professor of church music at Southern Baptist Seminary, Louisville, Kentucky, and author of* Jubilate! Church Music in the Evangelical Tradition.

# Appendix B

## Let's *at Least* Praise the Lord

### Charles H. Kraft

### 1989

IT'S PROBABLY AS OLD as the beginning of time. I suspect even Adam and Eve felt that "The younger generation is going to the dogs." And so we shouldn't be surprised if the same theme pops up with respect to "new" (or contemporary) church music. New things are always a threat to tradition. They mess up our ordinary ways of doing things! They require adjustment, rethinking, new learning. The new things don't seem to provide what we've learned to value in the old. And they introduce new considerations, some of which trouble us because we don't yet know how to control them.

The hymnbook has been an important part of evangelical church practice for generations. In fact, many of us, at least in the older generations, have used it so often in congregational singing that we have trouble imagining any other way to sing together in church. In addition, we have so often referred to what we do in church as "worship" that we have come to define the word "worship" as what we do during those times. It may seem heretical to suggest that there might be other legitimate ways keepers of tradition for someone to suggest such things as 1) that there might be other ways to sing together, 2) that what we do in church might not really be what worship was intended to be and, horror of horrors,

3) what we do with hymnbooks might even be counterproductive if worship is what we have in mind.

The threat to the hymnbook tradition that such suggestions raise seems to motivate Donald Hustad's article entitled, "Let's Not Just Praise the Lord" (CT Nov. 6, 1987; see Appendix A). Though every so often he tries to say something positive about "new" music, the overall impression is that praise and worship songs are unworthy in comparison to "real" worship music (i.e. that found in hymnbooks). It seems there is something very wrong with repetition, simplicity, accommodation and not using hymnbooks.

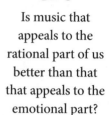

Is music that appeals to the rational part of us better than that that appeals to the emotional part?

The tone of the article is fearful, as if contemporary people who are being exposed to these modern songs are in danger of being misled into horrible heresy if they aren't taught to love the hymnbook.

Among the questions about the author's assumptions that the article raises in my mind are, Is the past always better than the present? Is music that appeals to the rational part of us better than that that appeals to the emotional and relational parts of us? Are didactic hymns automatically better than those that establish and carry a mood of worship? Are people so gullible that they're going to be ruined by a change in church music? Does "sacrifice of praise" require suffering?

## Who is the Audience?

Admittedly, any new thing needs to be looked at critically. But in my field, communication theory, we find it is important to specify just who is being talked to and who is being talked about. And Dr. Hustad doesn't make this clear. Does what he says about the threat of praise and worship music apply to all of the music in relation to all age groups? Or, is some of the "new" music okay for everyone and some okay just for some? His statements are global, all encompassing, designed to get us all to keep looking over our shoulders to guard against that ultimate tragedy when someone would abscond with all the hymnbooks and we'd be left with only praise and worship songs. How would anyone be able to learn anything then? And who would remember our marvelous heritage—Luther, the Reformation, "the traditional forms," organs, even Ambrose of Milan and somebody named Rhabanus Maurus?

I can think of at least two concerns that should give us pause lest we evaluate praise and worship music too harshly:

1. The first is *renewal.* The past is nice. But preservation of the past does not support renewal. And renewal is what the "new" music is all about, at least for many of us middle aged types. As an 80-year-old who's been in the church for over 70 of those years, I deeply appreciate the renewal I've been experiencing during the last thirty years—renewal in which praise and worship music has played an important part. Is that music dangerous for me and others like me?

   Renewal is what the new music is all about.

   In response to his article, I found myself wanting to shout, "Hey Dr. Hustad, some of us have discovered that Christianity is for the present! We've discovered that what God intended for us is not something that merely had a marvelous past and looks forward to a great future! God is alive to-day! IT'S RENEWAL TIME! CHRISTI-ANITY HAS BECOME EXCITING! For the first time in my life, I'm learning to really worship the God I've known for a long time but am now getting to know much better. Please don't take one of the primary vehicles of this renewal away from me." When the renewal dies down again the organs and hymnbooks will still be around.

   I'm learning to really worship.

2. The second concern is *relevance.* For many younger Christians, the key issue is not so much renewal as it is relevance. Many of those nurtured on the popular music of the latter half of the twentieth century (for better or worse), *need to have beat and contemporary instruments or they'll not be in church at all.*

Is it better to preserve the past and lose that group? Content? They get enough (maybe too much) of that in the sermons. Maybe there is some part of human-beingness that their elders never bothered to develop? Why should the devil have all the good music?, they ask. The organs and hymnbooks will still be around for any of them who decide to agree with their elders that emotion has no place in the church.

## I Love Hymns

You'd probably never guess it, but I love hymns, and organs. I have always *liked* them. But now, as I am being renewed, it's becoming full-fledged love (except when the organist forgets to help us worship and insists on showing off). The change began, however, as I started using the contemporary songs and, with their help, learning more of what praise and worship were intended to be.

I am learning from the contemporary music that praise is singing thankfully *about* God and worship is singing thankfully *to* God. I also am learning that praise and worship, like any kind of lovemaking, are intended to take time. I find that short, repetitious songs help me to learn the words so I can sing with my eyes closed and focus on God, not on reading words or notes. I am discovering that focusing on God, and especially on who He is and what He does today, gets my emotions in gear so that even when the sermon is overly rationalistic, it can't completely deprive me of worship. For, as I've observed elsewhere, "meanings are primarily felt, not reasoned" (see my book *Communication Theory for Christian Witness*, Orbis, 1991).

So now I get more out of most hymns too. I'm learning to worship and praise through them, as well as through worship and praise songs. But I had to find out what worship and praise were, through exposure to songs (and meanings) designed to serve that purpose before I could use hymns in that way. Unfortunately, my experience, and that of the majority of evangelicals with whom I've discussed the matter, is that hymnbook singing in ordinary

Now I get more out of hymns.

church contexts usually leaves us without feeling we have really worshipped. Indeed, most of us have grown up with very little understanding of what worship is supposed to be. It often tends to get confused with listening to sermons.

Who would ever guess from the average traditional evangelical church meeting that the hymn singing part was intended to be worshipful? If, as I contend, worship ought to be a form of lovemaking, who at the human level would settle for the kind of thing we do in church? Lovemaking takes time. And it cannot be done without getting our emotions into it. Nor can it be done effectively while reading a book. Singing from book only in the "cracks" between what are considered the more important parts of what we do when we're together on Sundays just doesn't do it. We would never get away with expressing our love to our spouses that way. Singing praisefully *about* and worshipfully *to* our God for half an hour to an hour at a time is, however, a totally different experience—especially if one doesn't have to read the words from a book at the same time.

## Forms and Their Meanings

There's a principle of communication that needs to be briefly developed here. For a more thorough treatment, see my book mentioned above. It's what we call the *"form-meaning principle."*

As humans, we exist in a cultural universe. This universe is structured into millions of non-material and material units called "cultural forms." Each custom is a cultural form made up of smaller cultural forms. Each part of language (e.g. words, grammar patterns) is a cultural form made up of smaller cultural forms. Each ritual (e.g. worship, wedding) is a cultural form made up of smaller cultural forms. Hymns, then, and praise songs also, are cultural forms that often function as parts of larger cultural forms called worship services.

But cultural forms do not carry their meanings with them. Meanings exist only in people. *People use and/or observe cultural forms and assign meaning to them on the basis of their own conditioning and habits of interpretation.* The interpretation assigned to some word or act by one person or group, therefore, may be quite different from that assigned to it by another person or group, especially if the two groups function on opposite sides of some social dividing line. This is why cultural forms such as hymns, and all other elements of ritual, take on different meanings for people of different generations and different experience. A music form that one group might interpret as conveying just the right meaning is often, therefore, interpreted by those of another generation or experience as conveying quite a different meaning.

With respect to a similar problem that existed in the early church, Paul articulated his conviction concerning this form-meaning principle by saying,

> People assign meaning on the basis of their habits of interpretation.

I am fully convinced that no food is unclean in itself. But if anyone regards something as unclean, then for him it is unclean (Rom. 14:14 NIV).

"Uncleanness" or "inappropriateness" are meanings attached by some people to certain cultural forms (e.g. drinking or refusing to drink certain beverages, using or refusing to use certain music). As Paul points out elsewhere in the chapter, then, we are as Christians to be very loving and considerate toward those who attach different meanings to forms we like/dislike.

A major problem arises when cultural forms are moved from one social group to another. For different social groups do not attach the same meanings to the same forms. When, for example, something is passed from one generation to another, we find that *the meanings attached to the cultural form by the receiving generation always differ to a greater or lesser extent from those attached*

> Music developed in one generation will mean something different in the next generation.

*to that form by the previous generation.* We can be certain, therefore, that hymns, or any other music, developed in one generation will mean something different to those of the next.

How, then, can we get the meanings that one generation attached to certain forms across to the members of the next generation? Only by discovering and using those forms within the new generation's experience to which they will attach similar meanings. It almost always requires different forms to convey the same meanings to those of different generations (or other social groupings), especially if, as in American society, the members of one generation have been taught to reject as much as possible of what the previous generation stands for. The principle is, *if the old forms are kept, the meanings will automatically be different. If the aim is to achieve continuity of meaning, then, new forms must be used.*

The operation of this principle is amply illustrated throughout the Scriptures. Many, if not all, of the rules of piety developed by the Pharisees, for example, were intended by the originating generation as genuine expressions of devotion to God. They were, however, *imposed* on succeeding generations of Pharisees who came to interpret them as means of attaining God's favor. The rules were also imposed on the common people, a social group over which the Pharisees exerted a certain amount of religious authority, and to them signified oppression. Rules and/or rituals (including hymns) that feel imposed mean something quite different from those voluntarily developed as expressions of what is already inside. The principle is further exemplified in the change in the meaning of the Law, the covenants, the Temple, the rituals and everything else that was passed from generation to generation in Scripture.

The preservation of the cultural forms of a past generation, no matter how vital they were to that generation, then, inevitably leads to deadness and lack of vitality within a generation or two. This principle has to be taken seriously at all points in the operation and communication of Christianity. It applies very obviously in the areas of worship and music, though it is easy for those who are brought up in and operate almost totally within the Christian ghetto to ignore this fact. When renewal happens, however, new worship and music forms are

To keep the meaning from generation to generation we must change the forms.

brought into being to express much the same kind of devotion as a previous generation expressed via the now outmoded worship and music forms.

## Teaching Versus Guiding Praise and Worship

At the time of the Reformation, and later in Wesley's day, ordinary church members were information-poor. Hymns, in addition to the function they served as vehicles for worship, were found to be very useful as teaching devices. So they were packed with doctrinal information.

Ours is a day, however, in which my generation participates in an information glut, both outside and inside the church. In the church we have been information-centered for so long that we tend to think there is something sacred about our tradition. In teaching, information is, of course, very necessary—but only in small doses. As Jesus knew (but most educational institutions don't seem to), information is deadly in large doses (see Jn. 16:12). He, therefore, refrained from overloading people with information. His teaching was event and story oriented (more like praise and worship music than like information-oriented hymns).

Traditional evangelical "worship" services center around the informationally-oriented sermon, preceded by a token number of informationally-oriented hymns, used largely as transitions between other components of the meeting. Besides being chock full of information and, therefore, very difficult to memorize, the hymns are usually in archaic language and thought forms, geared to other times, places, and interests. To sing them we have to glue our eyes to the book to read the fine print and sing to the floor. Any similarity between this kind of activity and worship is purely coincidental!

Praise and worship are quite a different matter. As mentioned above, praise and worship take time. It usually takes a lot of singing to create praise and worship. Chunks of time have to be set aside for it. Singing can't serve this purpose if it is merely crammed into cracks such as that between the Scripture reading and the sermon. If any given music is to create worship, it needs to come from the heart and be sung to the Lord, not to the floor—at least with heads up to the overhead screen.

I believe many in my generation are "over-hymned." we need the new music to help us develop the praise and worship dimension of our church life of which we have been deprived. True, we also need some teaching. But teaching we get in other contexts (e.g. preaching). Worship we get nowhere else. And hymns don't help many people with worship, I'm afraid.

Do we want information or stimulus in worship?

The younger generation, however, those brought up on praise and worship songs, is another matter. They may need more content in their music than they are getting. But they won't go to archaic hymns without a beat for that content. The music that will get that content across to contemporaries needs to be contemporary music. The values (meanings) of the past can only be gotten across through the forms of the present.

Does this generation, then, need new hymns? Is this generation again information-poor. Yes. Though the new hymns with more information in them than many of the praise and worship songs may need to be projected on screens via computers and power point, rather than merely recorded in hymnbooks. Probably the place to start in this process would be by producing verses to accompany some of the catchy praise songs already widely accepted. Another thing that can be done is to rework the music of at least some of the older hymns (as some contemporary music companies have started to do) so that those hymns make a positive impression on people conditioned by today's music styles. Such musical expression, then, may become the next phase in Christian music and even a new hymnology after the present praise and worship fad has itself passed into history.

## Cultural Forms Wear Out

As indicated above, cultural forms that are very meaningful for one generation or one group of people are often not very meaningful for another. This fact has nothing to do with whether or not the forms are, or once were "good" or appropriate. The "goodness" or appropriateness of a cultural form is always a matter of taste. And new generations are notorious for changing from the tastes of previous generations.

What is good music for one generation or social group may be disdained by another. Maximum attention, therefore, has to be given to accommodating to changes in taste by producing forms that will be regarded as appropriate by the receiving group. The question, then, is which forms should be used to attract, encourage and help to grow which people? The answer will differ from group to group. But the forms used must "belong" to the group using them. Decisions should be made, therefore, on the basis of what will most feel to a receiving group that it belongs to them, not on the basis of what tradition those in power like.

As I have said above, I like hymns. But lots of people are turned off and/or damaged by them. The turned off group includes many younger people. But there is also an older group who have been damaged by the exclusive use of hymns. Sadly, many of these would never guess there is much more to Christianity than they have been experiencing. Their Christian

What is "good" music for one generation may be poor for the next.

practice has been so affected by the lack of vitality in the so-called "worship services" they attend that they often cannot imagine anything different, anything alive.

Some of these "oldies," however, are quite alive and find that hymn singing feeds this aliveness. They may be blessed by being part of a congregation with creative music/worship leaders. Or they may be new converts, who even archaic language, thought forms and music cannot dissuade from vitality. Or they may be professional keepers of tradition who, either in addition to or alongside of carrying out their mandate to preserve the past, are experiencing their relationship with Christ in a vital way. Or they may, through exposure to praise and worship music and the kind of worship experience that often accompanies it, be living in renewal and, therefore, find quite exciting and helpful many of the hymnbook expressions of spirituality.

So, for one group we dare not recommend hymns. For another, however, they're helpful. How, then, should we come to an opinion concerning them? The opinion needs to be based on the kind of ministry in which the hymns are to participate and the kind of people the ministry seeks to reach. Is that ministry one that aims to reach contemporary people? God cares for contemporary people and would like to see them presented with His messages in as attractive a way as possible. Use contemporary music.

Is it a ministry that seeks to preserve an aging flock who would be disturbed rather than renewed if anyone tampered with the music? God cares whether these people are helped or hindered. Out of love for them any change needs to be slow. But often these people need new vitality in their Christian experience. Judicious interweaving of praise and worship songs into hymn-based worship may be acceptable and helpful. The primary change, however, should probably be to help them to discover what worship is by spending longer periods of time in singing (especially *to* God). This should be accompanied by interpretation and instruction concerning worship—sermons teaching people about worship.

Or are we talking about a ministry that, like most, involves audiences that are a mixture of the above two types of people (plus perhaps others)? We need to learn to use all kinds of music for such audiences, recognizing that it is the meaning as determined by the various receiving groups that is crucial, not the mere preserving of forms that once served their purpose well.

But people need interpretation of what is going on. Those who prefer one form of music need to be taught what those who prefer another kind are feeling when their taste is being served. Look at the looks on their faces as they sing their preferred music. Each group needs to learn to appreciate the

Look at the looks on their faces as they sing their preferred music.

importance of the other music to the group who prefers it. God loves people. And He made people with a great deal of diversity.

To love and serve people, then, means to love and serve them in their diversity.

But whatever the situation, *let's learn to worship*. Let's learn to make love to God. Let's not just preserve for the sake of preserving or change for the sake of changing. Let's stop being enslaved to the present rationalistic, intellect-centered approach to church that characterizes most of evangelicalism. Sadly, what we call "worship services" often contain no worship at all. Worship takes time. And it gets the emotions in gear. It is expressive, not passive. It is relation centered, not intellect centered. If it provides food for the intellect, well and good. But too much food for the intellect kills other valid parts of the intellect owners. Let the sermon still be important. But let worship, real worship, be just as focal.

Let's not *just* praise the Lord. But let's *at least* praise (and worship) Him!

# Appendix C

## The Hymnbook is Not Enough

### Charles H. Kraft

[Published in *Christianity Today*,
April 7, 1989]

NEW THINGS OFTEN THREATEN tradition. It should not surprise us
if that even applies to new church music especially the use of praise
songs in worship. But many of us desperately need new worship
music to rejuvinate our spiritual lives and revitalize our worship.
And if we hope to meet the needs of our young people and attract
the unchurched--the music will get Christian content across to
contemporary people in contemporary music.

Because of the place of hymnals in our evangelical traditions, we may be unable to imagine worship without them. But it
is tradition, not Scripture, that makes it seem heretical to suggest
that there are other ways to sing together, and that what we do in
church might even be counterproductive to worship.

While I have always enjoyed singing in church, it wasn't until
I freed myself from exclusive use of the hymnal that I experienced
what praise and worship can be. And it is the new music, sung
with eyes closed for 10, 15, or 20 minutes at a time, that makes that
experience possible. These short, repetitious songs with memo-
rable, pictureful lyrics help me focus on God. I don't even need
to look at the music. The pleasant result is that now I am learning

to worship and praise through hymns, as well as through worship and praise songs.

Unfortunately, many of us have grown up with very little understanding of worship. Our worship services revolve around an informational sermon preceded by a token number of informational hymns. Our hymns are often little more than transitional devices between other parts of the service.

Besides spending too little time singing, we sing hymns so chock-full of rational content and information that they are un-memorizable. In addition, the hymns are usually written in archaic language and thought forms geared to other times, places, and interests. To sing them, we glue our eyes to the hymnal and sing to the floor.

True worship involves something quite different. It usually takes a lot of singing to create an atmosphere of praise and worship. Singing cannot serve this purpose if it is crammed between the offering, Scripture reading and sermon. If any music is to foster worship, it should come from the heart and be sung to the Lord, not to the floor.

We also need to realize that styles that are meaningful for one generation or one group of people are often not very meaningful for another. To live out our commission to love and serve people means to love and serve them in their great diversity. Even when it comes to music.

Is the main audience made up of younger people? Contemporary music should predominate. Is it a largely older congregation, one that would be disturbed if anyone tampered with the music? Even for such a group, the worshipfulness of their experience could be enhanced by spending more time in singing (especially singing to God). And if we're discussing a ministry that, like most, serves a mixture of those two groups (and others) we need to open our services to all kinds of music.

Remember, however, that people need to understand what is happening. We should accompany our changes with instructions that helps people understand the meaning of worship, and we should strive always to keep our focus in worship on God. And those who prefer one form of music need to learn to empathize with those who prefer something quite different.

Whatever the situation, let's stop being enslaved to the rationalistic, intellect-centered approach to church that characterizes much of evangelicalism. Worship takes time. It is expressive, not passive. It is, after all, the outpouring of a relationship. Let's not just sing; let's praise, and make worship the focal point of our services.